# THE TV-GUIDED AMERICAN

*Also by the author:*

LI'L ABNER:
A Study in American Satire

THE COMIC-STRIPPED AMERICAN

# THE TV-GUIDED AMERICAN

## ARTHUR ASA BERGER

**WALKER AND COMPANY**

**NEW YORK**

*In memory of my mother and father*

# foreword

Arthur Asa Berger's *Comic-Stripped American* has proved to be an ideal prelude to *The TV-guided American*. The icons of the comic-strip world invite the same kind of *figure/ground* analysis as the TV images. That is to say, both comics and TV are not entirely visual forms of managing experience and publics. When I wrote *The Mechanical Bride* in the 1940's (not published until 1951), America was still deeply embedded in the primarily visual forms of movies and journalism. In fact, *The Mechanical Bride* barely made it before she was superseded by the electronic bride of the TV age.

Professor Berger keeps in mind both the old visual, specialized and mechanical culture and also the new multi-sensuous electronic culture. The TV-guided American is worlds away from the old movie-guided American, since the TV-guided American is a person who has undergone

not merely all the programs and advertisements of recent decades but the re-education of his sensuous and perceptual life. Professor Berger cites *The Responsive Chord* of Tony Schwartz who tells us that "watching TV, the eye is for the first time functioning like the ear" (p. 16). This sensory education proceeds quite regardless of the programs, and has transformed young America. The programmers have responded intuitively to the new medium and its deeply involving character, with a variety of strategies which are often based on audience research and ratings. The entertainer has always been able to tune in his public without any aid from sociology or conceptual patterning. He "puts on" his public as the shaping force of his expression. Baudelaire put the reciprocal relation in a single phrase: "Hypocrite lecteur, mon semblable, mon frère." And Joyce, likewise: "My consumers, are they not my producers?" Since America, more than any country, began with a commitment to visual technology, the veering, subliminally, of American sensibilities from visual to acoustic structure has become a revolution, both in personal identity and in social and political forms.

Professor Berger shows us some of the main problems and patterns of Western man in the electric age in the course of studying TV programs from *All in the Family* to *Monty Python's Flying Circus*. One of his persistent themes is rapidly changing problem of identity, both private and corporate. This tends to be inseparable from the problems of goals and objectives, both private and national. Politically, the problem peers at us from the countenance of Archie Bunker. Archie has no outer goals, but many inner anxieties. In the section on *Kung Fu*, Professor Berger introduces us to the American fascination with Eastern culture, reminding us that the entire Western world has been

moving Eastward for some time, even as the entire Oriental world has been moving Westward. The West moves inward and Eastward via electric circuitry, while the East moves Westward and outward via the old hardware and machinery of the West.

Apropos *Gunsmoke*, Professor Berger tells us: "The problem of the Western is why it is so popular and what it tells us about American culture and character." As usual, he moves to the center of the problem of American identity. Visually oriented man is necessarily a *figure* without a *ground*. He has no roots. In a hostile world he goes outside to be alone and goes home to be social, thus reversing the pattern of mankind. The motor car is the supreme form of American identity since it enables us to be private when outside. TV threatens the psychological meaning of the car, since TV brings the outside inside the home which is friendly and communal. TV threatens both the car and the Western, as well as all the other symbols of American identity. If the phonetic alphabet fissioned the visual faculty out from the other senses, creating Western man and the aggressive carriers of the Western way from Euclid to "Mistah Kurtz" (Conrad's *The Heart of Darkness*), then the TV image reverses this process, putting the visual faculty back in the complex of the senses.

The TV-guided American is being hoicked out of the Western pattern and returned to a universal way of life which has few, if any, of the components of visual space and order. Professor Berger enables us to observe many of the effects and side effects of being a TV-guided American.

— Marshall McLuhan

# contents

# introduction

In only two decades of massive national experience television has transformed the political life of the nation, has changed the daily habits of our people, has molded the style of the generation, made overnight global phenomena of local happenings, redirected the flow of information and values from traditional channels into centralized networks reaching into every home. In other words, it has profoundly affected what we call the process of socialization, the process by which members of our species become human.

> —GEORGE GERBNER
> from testimony before the
> National Commission on the
> Causes and Prevention
> of Violence.

1

The first television program I can remember seeing was the Joe Louis/Jersey Joe Wolcott fight. I was just a youngster and my family didn't have a set, but a neighbor did and he invited some of us to watch the fight with him. He had one of the first sets—one that could not have been more than eight inches in diameter but, to us, awestruck by the magic of it all, it seemed gigantic. Very few people had them at the time, and they were very expensive.

And yet, a generation later, almost all households have sets in America, and these sets are incredibly cheap. Black-and-white television sets can be purchased for as little as seventy or eighty dollars, so that many families have two or three sets, and a large number of people have color sets, the miracle of miracles. The average person is so addicted to television that if his set does not work, he will have his old one fixed, or buy a new one, within three days.

A new generation has been raised in America—a generation that doesn't know what life can be like without television and can't seem to imagine what life is like without it.

The statistics about television use are staggering. In the typical household, the television set is on an average of at least five hours a day. It is estimated that the average young person watches some 22,000 hours of television by the time he finishes high school, and is exposed to something in the neighborhood of 600,000 commercials during this period. These figures mean that a typical American child spends the equivalent of almost three years of his life watching television.

No wonder S. I. Hayakawa has said (in an extremely suggestive article, "Who's Bringing Up Your Children?"): Since children are spending something like three years out

of their lives—that is one-sixth of their lives between birth and eighteen—watching television, these are three years in which they are not having time to play with peers, interact with their parents, read, or have fantasies, though they are able to do *some* of these things at the same time they watch.

Television, obviously, plays an enormous role in socializing our children. It teaches them roles to play; it provides them with heroes to emulate and imitate; it gives them information about the world and has produced a generation of young people who are extremely knowledgeable in certain ways. But it also exposes them to violence and other socially undesirable phenomena, whose consequences many people fear are destructive to their wellbeing. It may be a coincidence, but the first television generation is also the first hard-drugs generation—and I happen to believe that there is a connection, which has to do with the enormous amount of drug advertising we see on television and what I call the pain-pill-pleasure model, which we find in many of the drug commercials.

What I'm suggesting is that television is a way of knowing, a way of learning about the world, about how to fit into it, what it has to offer, and so on. It provides role models; it confers identity; it offers people subjects for conversation and may be one of the few unifying factors in American culture.

We have always learned by looking—that is, in fact, the basis of the scientific method. Observation is a fundamental way of knowing (in the West at least), and the elaborate experiments of scientists are essentially attempts at securing better and more systematic observation. But with television the observation is diffused. You become

overwhelmed by the variety of things available, so that it frequently becomes impossible to organize the information you get from television and learn from it. Often we become confused, dazed. We are overwhelmed, and in such a state we become more susceptible to being influenced by it.

Radio is a way of knowing, also. You can learn from listening, which is, in fact, the traditional manner that students are taught in school. But television combines hearing with seeing, creating the most effective medium we have for attracting and keeping attention. It may even be that one of the problems we face in schools nowadays is that our children are so used to being entertained and stimulated by television that when they enter the schoolroom or university, they suffer from a kind of sensory deprivation. They are so used to being hopped up—and having the power to change channels the moment they are bored—that school becomes unbearable. They are understimulated and find schools intolerable.

There are certain things about television that explain the effect it has upon us. I have already commented on the amount of television we watch. It is by far the most important and most influential medium in this respect, for what it lacks in intensity it makes up for in volume.

One thing we must not forget is that the images we see are all miniatures. Even in the largest sets the figures are all greatly reduced. This is considerably different from what we see in the movies, for example. There we are overwhelmed by the size of the figures and almost absorbed by them. With television, however, we become Gullivers and the figures we watch are Lilliputians.

We also generally watch television in a lighted room, to reduce eyestrain, so that television does not have our un-

divided attention in the way movies do. While watching television we can answer phone calls, eat, even talk (though we do not converse as a rule). In short, the total commitment we make in the movie house or theater is not made when we watch television, especially if we are watching it in our own homes.

In addition to this miniaturization, which forces us, even though we may be unaware of what we are doing, to assign a secondary kind of reality status to the television images, television programs are almost always segmented. Every ten minutes or so in all programs, except those on public television, there are two, three, or more advertisements, which interrupt the continuity of the program. The average American learns, quickly, to distrust these commercials and mistakenly believes he is unaffected by them. I would suggest that we are affected by all communications, even though frequently appeals are made that influence us in ways we cannot fathom. In such cases our unconscious reacts—even though we may think, and believe, nothing is happening to us.

As Ernest Dichter, the eminent motivation researcher, puts it, "Whatever your attitude toward modern psychology or psychoanalysis, it has been proved beyond any doubt that many of our daily decisions are governed by motivations over which we have no control and of which we are often quite unaware." We frequently have the illusion that we are in complete control of ourselves and the contents of our minds and psyches; and it is this illusion that makes it possible for us to be manipulated all the more successfully.

From the advertisements, then, the average viewer learns that he cannot believe everything he sees. (We know that even children as young as seven do not trust commer-

cials, but they, too, are influenced by them.) The viewer learns that illusion is possible and that he must be on guard against it, even though, frequently, he *can see things for himself.* The problem is that *what* he sees is mediated by someone else; and though the viewer may see truth, he may not be seeing the whole truth.

Television also breaks up time in rather strange ways. Things can keep repeating themselves over and over again, so that you can move through time backward and "capture" the past. Many people have commented how strange it was seeing former President Nixon resigning from office again and again. The normal flow of time was disturbed; life took on a strange, somewhat surrealistic quality, and people seemed to be living in an eternal present. And as time loses its significance, space loses its meaning.

Distances become meaningless and, with our sense of time and space disturbed, we are forced into a radical alteration of the way we sense and understand the world. Marshall McLuhan has commented on this; he believes that television is making the world a "global village," since we now have instantaneous communications linking all parts of the world together.

Thus, we find that the form of television has a great deal of importance and affects the way we judge its contents. Segmented, miniature images cannot possibly have the power over us that uninterrupted gigantic images do, but what television loses as a medium because of its nature, it more than makes up because of its popularity. It dominates the leisure time of the American public. The average American family probably spends more time watching television in a week than it does watching films in a month or a year.

I have discussed the power and influence of television as a medium because these factors are basic to my argument. This book is about the cultural significance of some of the important television programs. I believe that programs such as *Mission Impossible, Star Trek, Gunsmoke* and *Kung Fu,* are worth looking at carefully because they reflect certain American values and because they probably have also helped reinforce many people's notions about what the good life is, what it is to be a man or woman, what heroism means, and so on.

Although there are many books about television as a medium, there has been relatively little attention paid to the cultural significance of various television programs. If you think, for example, of the difference between television criticism and movie criticism, you will see what I'm talking about. The cinema, which in recent years has come to be looked upon as an art form, is given serious attention by its critics, who write searching and sometimes rather obscure essays about the more important films.

Of course, the very fact that television is so ubiquitous, that on any given day in a typical metropolitan area some hundreds of programs are shown, makes it difficult to take television seriously. There is a curious tendency in people to neglect things that are part of their everyday life. The very accessibility of television tends to make us dismiss it from serious consideration. How, we ask, can anything be important if millions of people are doing it every day?

In sum, television, relatively speaking, has not been given the serious attention it deserves—either by the press or by the intellectual or academic community. The average newspaper has a great deal more film criticism—if that's what you want to call it—than television criticism. Why

is this so? Why should the most important and powerful medium of our day be neglected this way? Because we see it as a kind of entertainment that is not worth bothering with, for one reason; and because, as I have suggested, we tend to undervalue what is easily obtainable. Many a young man travels the world in search of his ideal love, only to find her (and this is a typical theme in television stories) in the girl next door.

I have selected a number of programs that I consider relevant and have written about their cultural significance. What do they reveal about American character? What important themes—such as desexualization, dehumanization, alienation—do we find in them? What roles do they focus on? What do they suggest is normal? How do they use or abuse sexuality? It is the cultural richness of a program that attracts me; I make no defense for my selection other than that I believe it is worth looking into—as well as at.

When you decide to write a book, and in particular a book on a medium like television, enormous problems immediately present themselves. After all, television has been going strong for thirty years, and there have been thousands of different series in all kinds of different formats. As I sat writing this book, a bewildering and amazing assortment of programs were appearing on television. It immediately became apparent to me that I could not cover everything— and, indeed, that it is not necessary to do so. There have been excellent books written on news broadcasting, children's television, and various other aspects of the medium.

What I decided to do was write a book much like my *The Comic-Stripped American* (New York: Walker and Company, 1973). I have selected a number of programs and subjected them to scrutiny. I cannot claim that my

selection is "scientific" in the narrowest sense of the term, or that everyone will find himself or herself agreeing with what I have written. I have chosen programs that most people are familiar with and will consider important, and I have things to say that will help you see these programs in a new light. By extension, you will also see American culture and perhaps even yourself differently. We are what we eat—and in a similar sense, we also are what we see—though all too frequently we are unaware of the full significance of what it is that we eat and see, or afraid to admit to ourselves their importance.

Yet, the very terms we give television—the boob tube, the one-eyed babysitter,—all indicate an uneasy sense that television has a power over us, or a role in our lives, that we are reluctant to acknowledge. To recapitulate: strictly speaking, it is not television per se, as a medium, but certain kinds of programs that I am interested in. People talk about television rather loosely—it is a term that encompasses news programs, sports programs, advertisements, situation comedies, space operas, detective and crime adventures, westerns, a whole world (or wasteland) of all kinds of different programs that we subsume under the general term "television."

In actuality, television is a medium that does what all media do—it *carries* a number of different forms of popular culture, and it really is these programs that are critical. So this book is about television, but in a rather special way. It is about television programs, which is actually what we mean, really, when we talk about watching television. We ask a friend, "Did you see _____ on television last night?" Or, "Did you watch television?" But we always talk about what was on the news or a specific program, because people

are not interested in commenting upon the medium and its social significance. Rather, they want to talk about specific programs that they liked or did not like, found interesting or dull.

It is these programs carried on television that we will examine now. Some of us, who have been on television, are televised Americans. But we are all, with rare exceptions, TV guided Americans—people who have followed *Batman* or *All in the Family* or *Kung Fu,* sometimes for a number of years. Why we did, and what we got out of them, are what remains for us to find out.

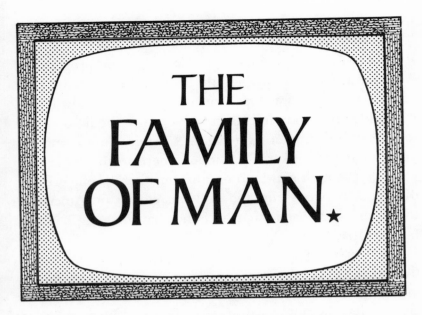

# THE FAMILY OF MAN ★

## ★ the ethnic joke as situation comedy

Every situation comedy extant owes fealty to Archie and Edith Bunker and to Mike and Gloria. In one smashing, revolutionary opening half-hour (January, 1971), they destroyed old taboos and liberated television comedy writing.

The nation's critics caught on instantly. The public didn't latch on until the summer reruns, 13 weeks later. The public never let loose. Archie Bunker was a bigot but he was real. The family and neighborhood forces battering him were real. The situations—ranging from female menopause to male impotency, from communism to racism—were unparalleled in television comedy. They were shocking, startling and often uproariously funny.

—DWIGHT NEWTON
*San Francisco Sunday*
*Examiner & Chronicle*
October 27, 1974

*All in the Family* is the most popular television program in America and has been a family favorite here for the past few years, since it was first shown in January, 1971. There is considerable irony in this situation, since the hero of the series, Archie Bunker, is a bigot. A crude, dumb, and ignorant fellow, Bunker is a symbolic hero in the American pantheon of fools and loudmouths, but there is one critical difference between him and previous clowns on American television, and that is that he is not harmless, he has not been sanitized.

*All in the Family* is really a case study in the demythologizing of the American working classes. In the popular mind, the working-class blue collar worker is seen as a clean-living, honest, hard-working person who is tolerant of his fellowman, God-fearing, perhaps a bit materialistic, but generally speaking a fine figure. This heroic figure, the so-called common man, has traditionally been seen as a reservoir of good sense and an upholder of our democratic values. This is the way the common man is presented in the media, at least.

Curiously enough, this same fantasy of the innate goodness of the common man, a legacy of our past (when the country was filled with nature's noblemen) is kept alive by certain elements of the political left, who have a vested interest in the proletariat as the redeemers of a bourgeois American civilization that has lost its way and is destructive of man's humanity. Jefferson said:

> State a moral case to a ploughman and a professor. The former will decide it as well, and often better than the latter, because he has not been led astray by artificial rules.

We believe that the common man will save us because he is closer to nature and to life. This notion is connected with

our egalitarianism and our anti-intellectualism, our fear of
institutions and our defining ourselves as "natural" as con-
trasted to "civilized," a subject I will discuss in greater detail later.

In any case, Archie Bunker does not seem to be very
noble, and his description of his fellow Americans seems
far removed from what we might expect from the natural
democrat. To quote the beginning of a *Newsweek* article,
"TV: Speaking About the Unspeakable" (Nov. 29, 1971):

> Archie Bunker, the middle American hero of *All in the
> Family,* speaks what was utterly unspeakable on televi-
> sion before him. He sees himself menaced by a rising tide
> of spades, spics, spooks, schwartzes, coons, coloreds, Chinks,
> Commies and their Commie crapola, jungle bunnies, jigs,
> pinkos, pansies, hebes, yids, black beauties, bleeding hearts,
> tamale eaters, yentas, atheists, weirdos, dumb Polacks,
> dingbats, meatheads, fairies, fruits, fags, and four-eyes.
> These are the words he uses in a medium that usually
> minces words to the consistency of toddler food.

There seems to be an endless number of people whom
Archie hates, and American audiences seem to derive a
great deal of pleasure from seeing and hearing Archie vent
his wrath upon various scapegoats.

On the basis of this listing it seems obvious that Archie
feels threatened by almost everyone around him, and is
suffering from a kind of diffuse paranoia. The family of man
is myth; everyone is a menace. Now, since the program is
bathed in a kind of gruff geniality and since Archie is a fool,
we don't take it all as seriously as we might. But many a
word said in jest is an honest representation of people's
feelings, and we cannot let the comedy completely obscure
the aggression beneath it.

Archie is trapped and frustrated; he is locked into a

dead-end job, like many Americans, and reacts to this by blaming others for his situation. He was told, like all Americans, that the future was his—if only he had the willpower. And it might have all worked out, were it not for all the Jews and coons and other people corrupting American society.

When you scratch the typical working-class person, and dig beneath the thin veneer of elementary school civics he carries around in his head, you find things to make you shudder. Let me quote, in this respect, from Seymour Martin Lipset's classic, *Political Man*. Discussing the typical lower-class individual, Lipset says:

> He is likely to have been exposed to punishment, lack of love, and a general atmosphere of tension and aggression since early childhood—all experiences which tend to produce deep-rooted hostilities expressed by ethnic prejudices, political authoritarianism, and chiliastic transvaluational [pie in the sky when you die] religion. His educational attainment is less than that of men with higher socio-economic status, and his association as a child with others of a similar background not only fails to stimulate his own intellectual interests but also creates an atmosphere which prevents his educational experience from increasing his general social sophistication and his understanding of different groups and ideas. Leaving school rather early, he is surrounded on the job by others with a similarly restricted cultural, educational, and family background.

If you think of it, *All in the Family* can be looked upon as a kind of ethnic joke that has been expanded into a situation comedy. In the case of *All in the Family*, the fact that Archie's son-in-law is Polish facilitates the whole mat-

ter, for in the program Mike Stivic actually is (to people sympathetic with Archie) a "Polish joke."

Ethnic humor has been around for a long time! Since the first man noticed he was different from the second, and ethnocentrism first appeared, ethnic jokes must have been popular. The Greeks had ethnic jokes about the uncouth Romans, the Romans had ethnic jokes about the uncouth barbarians, and the Chinese probably had ethnic jokes about everybody. Jokes feed on differences and distinctions, and if one of the functions of ethnic jokes is to ridicule others, another function (and one which we are seldom aware of) is to maintain a sense of one's ethnicity, and with it, identity.

America, as a nation of immigrants—each with different customs and traditions and values—is, par excellence, a breeding house of ethnic jokes. The jokes help *release aggression without guilt,* and as such, have no doubt been instrumental in facilitating the relatively stable mixing of different ethnic groups in America.

We realize, of course, that America is not a mixing or melting pot. Rather, different groups have lived side-by-side, often with an uneasy toleration (at best) of one another. Telling jokes about other ethnic groups is a good way to let off steam; verbal aggression becomes a substitute for physical aggression. It is cheaper and the results are almost guaranteed.

Ethnic humor, as a manifestation of ethnocentrism, is generally built upon stereotypes—vague and usually absurd notions people have about other people, frequently picked up from the mass media, but also learned from family, school, and social experiences. The jokes tend to reinforce the stereotypes in the minds of the teller, even

though he realizes they are absurd and incorrect. This is because we generally believe there is a core of truth to stereotypes, even though they may not be nice.

There is a question as to whether ethnic humor is, in fact, ethnic—that is, whether it is aimed at the ethnicity (and distinctive qualities) of groups or their socio-economic status. It may very well be, for example, that the jokes about Polaks, Wops, Yids, Micks, and others, may *really* be attacks on their lower-class life styles and not ethnic peculiarities. Perhaps Americans associate dirtiness, cowardice, uncouth behavior, vulgarity, and other distasteful qualities, with classes beneath them, and just single out different nationalities to represent assigned vices.

Ethnic jokes may represent the opposite of ascribed status; they are *ascribed deflation,* which gain currency because the jokes are comic and release aggression in a fairly economical and harmless way. This deflation may be the key to comedy, for as Hobbes says in *The Leviathan*:

> The passion of laughter is nothing else but sudden glory arising from a sudden conception of some eminency in ourselves by comparison with the infirmity of others, or with our own formerly.

We take comfort in the relative deprivation of status that we inflict upon others. This would lead us to believe that there is an element of status anxiety involved in ethnic jokes—both in the kinds told about others and the kinds ethnic groups tell about themselves.

This explains the significance of a figure like Archie Bunker, the supposedy "lovable bigot." He is full of ethnic prejudices and bigotry, but because he is dumb and a clown figure (he makes all kinds of malapropisms and log-

ical errors), we don't seem to take his bigotry seriously and can find him funny, and in some way endearing. The reason some people reject ethnic jokes is because the aggression in them is too overt; when that happens, and the aggressive content is not adequately masked, the joke falls flat and our superego, no longer tricked, comes into action and pricks our conscience.

With Archie Bunker we get a double payoff, so to speak. We are able to enjoy the ethnic humor, in one sense, and condemn it in another. And by making Archie Bunker ridiculous (or by telling infantile Polish and other ethnic joke-riddles) we minimize the aggressive aspect of this humor. It is as if to say, "But don't take this seriously, please!"—which happens to be the truth. The point is that we can get the forbidden pleasure of aggression against ethnic groups and the pleasure of aggression against the aggressor, and so get twice as much pleasure for our money —or time spent—and we come out smelling like the proverbial rose. Or do we?

One of the most controversial aspects of the program involves the effects of *All in the Family* upon the American public. The producer of the program argues that it pokes fun at bigotry and brings it out into the open, where it can be observed and condemned. Those who attack the program say that having Archie a lovable bigot actually serves to reinforce prejudice and condone bigotry. Until recently the social scientists had not become involved with the argument, but a recent issue of the *Journal of Communication* carried a compelling article on the matter. Entitled "Archie Bunker's Bigotry: A Study in Selective Perception and Exposure," authors Neil Vidmar and Milton Rokeach reported the results of a survey made in America and

Canada. Shortly after the program began, CBS made a telephone survey of viewer opinion of the program. This survey reported that most of the viewers perceived the program's satirical intents so its impact would be to reduce prejudice.

Vidmar and Rokeach are not certain such is the case:

> There is, however, an alternative hypothesis which might explain why the program was enjoyed by the great majority of viewers. Perhaps prejudiced and unprejudiced persons ascribe different meanings to the intent and outcomes of *All in the Family* episodes: nonprejudiced viewers and minority group viewers may perceive and enjoy the show as satire, whereas prejudiced viewers may perceive and enjoy the show as episodes "telling it like it is." Such a hypothesis seems to be supported by the fact that some viewers write letters (to newspaper editors, to CBS officials, and to people associated with the program) which applaud Archie for his racist viewpoint, while others applaud the show for effectively making fun of bigotry.

Different people view the program in different ways; both bigots and nonbigots see the show as supporting their particular points of view. As a result of an empirical survey the authors concluded, finally, that the program is harmful:

> On balance the study seems to support more the critics who have argued that *All in the Family* has harmful effects. Some serious questions have been raised by these critics. Both Hobson and Slawson have asserted that by making Archie a "lovable bigot" the program encourages bigots to excuse and rationalize their own prejudices. Sanders has charged that "already there is evidence that impressionistic white children have picked up and are using, many of the old racial slurs which Archie has resurrected, popularized and made 'acceptable' all over again." Our empirical re-

search suggests that at the very least those charges have a valid psychological base.

It is not hard to agree with the authors if you know anything about satire, for large numbers of people are unable to recognize that something is being satirized. Young children don't see the satirical intent in *Batman,* and unsophisticated sensibilities cannot recognize the satire in *All in the Family.* Whatever the case, though, it is obvious that large numbers of people are deriving pleasure (of varying sorts) from the program.

It is interesting to compare *All in the Family* with the program which it is modelled upon, *Till Death Us Do Part.* This program was originated in England in 1966, by the British Broadcasting Corporation, and it has not only spawned *All in the Family* in America, but a legion of similar programs in other countries.

There are similarities between the two programs but also considerable differences.

*Till Death Us Do Part* has been the most popular English television comedy of the past few years—and certainly one of the most popular television programs of this period. It is now in its fourth series and still going strong, though some of the critics have suggested that it may have outlived its usefulness and no longer is as funny or remarkable as it once was. I can't judge the merits of these criticisms because I have not seen the other three series, but even my limited viewing of the most recent episodes is enough for me to grasp that it is a remarkable program.

What we find is a genuine *grotesque,* Alf Garnett, who fights endlessly with his wife, another grotesque (but a much more humanized one than Alf), his daughter and son-

in-law, and all the forces of liberalism in England—such as the Labour Party, his pet hate.

The title of the show is most ambivalent. It has something to do with the marriage contract and with marriage conflict. There is a little world of people who share a small, run-down apartment and who fight, like children, about everything. It is a kind of fight to the death, a blood feud between members of the same family who enjoy it all, who can't avoid the cutting remark or the practical joke, who love and hate each other a great deal.

Alf Garnett is, like Archie Bunker, "a working-class authoritarian." He is a bigot, a racist who has contempt for Jews, Negroes, colored people, and members of the Labour Party, whom he calls "bloody wogs." He, himself, is a study in contradiction—a working-class Tory, who can't understand what the members of the Conservative Party are talking about, but whose habits of deference carry him on. He digs the fancy types who would find him absolutely loathsome, and he wears a homburg to complement his cheap National Health Service glasses.

He is a grotesque, whose grotesquery mirrors the distortions in the society in which he finds himself. He fascinates, perhaps because he forces us, in some strange way, to see ourselves. Monsters like Alf, full of rage and fury, reflect all of us—how we would like to be able to insult people, to "vent our spleen" at people we don't like, to be irrational and luxuriate in malicious and absurd hatred. Alf is pure feeling in a country full of up-tight people with monstrous superegoes, who cannot let themselves go and express their feelings, whether generous or not. There is a great deal of tension in the air in England over the matter of aggression (which explains why darts and the hunt are

so popular), and in this carefully preserved sea of nervous tranquility old Alf Garnett is thrashing about, screaming bloody murder, a brilliant antihero who has the luxury of being able to hate—and, as a corollary, being able to feel. *In a country full of repressed hysterics, Alf Garnett is the ego-ideal of millions.*

They don't know this, of course. And he pays a price —he is a fool, nobody takes him seriously, people laugh at him. Actually he provides a number of gratifications for his followers. As I suggested above, he speaks for their secret souls, which would like to be free to admit their hatred (at times, at least) of people. But we get a double payoff from him, as well as Archie. In addition to getting, vicariously, the forbidden pleasure of aggression against ethnic groups and political parties we don't like through Alf, we then get the added pleasure of feeling legitimate aggression against Alf, the aggressor. He gives us good value for money.

What, we may ask, is the source of Alf's energy? What fuels his rage? I can only offer a guess, but I sense it is the result of frustration, the result of his being a petty and powerless figure, locked like his confrere into a dead-end job with no sense of the future. It is a consequence of *stasis* —there is no tomorrow for Alf in the sense that tomorrow will be no different from today. He is perfectly secure within the confines of his little world, which helps explain why he is so open and obvious. He is at the bottom of the totem pole and doesn't have to worry about offending anyone and losing face.

And yet, underneath the rage, underneath the hate lavished on Wogs and the Labour Party and the whole intellectual elite of liberal or radical persuasion, there is a

diffuse sense of terror in old Alf. He is stuck in his own Hell (which, as Sartre said, is "other people"), and he cannot justify his life, or English politics, except by finding scapegoats, sacrificial victims who have invaded the paradise that was England and prevented the policies of the Conservative Party from working. (The tragedy of the working people in America is that too many of them hate and not enough of them vote. Alf, at least, I suspect is not caught in that bind.)

Alan Coren of *The Times* has recognized this static quality in the show and criticized it:

> Nothing happens. The great creation remains locked in his East End parlour, loggerheaded with his monster family, and waits for some news to break upon which his now familiar spleen can be predictably vented.

He concludes that "Alf has become a bore," and suggests that Johnny Speight, who writes the show, "must make him do, not just let him be." I would not agree, for the genius of the fool is in being and not doing. The creation of contrived situations would diminish and dilute Alf's personality. Situation comedy rests on the triumph of situation over individuality and personality; anyone, placed in certain situations, becomes comic. A great character like Alf must *be* comic and not be made comic.

The humor in the program is essentially verbal and is based on insults, revelation of ignorance, facetiousness, sarcasm, and repartee. Dandy Nichols, who plays the wife (and who is a much stronger figure than her American counterpart) is a superb actress and is a perfect foil for Alf. She is a master of the disdainful glance and the nasty repartee. In one program which was based on a practical joke—the idea

that his wife had not made his evening meal—there was the following conversation. Alf complained about not liking cheese sandwiches.

ALF: "I'm not a bloody mouse!"
WIFE: "I wish you were . . . I'd set a trap for you."

There was also a scene in which Alf tried to get a word in edgewise some six or eight times, but each time he said "Look . . ." his wife interrupted him and rambled on.

The acting is generally quite superb and it helps to carry the program. It also is very topical and manages to focus upon some critical event in the political scene each week as it rolls along. Oil, the three-day week, for example, are all grist for its militancy. We cannot be sure that the best lack all conviction, but in Alf Garnett, we can have good reason to suspect that the worst are full of passionate intensity.

It is obvious that *All in the Family* is much softer and weaker than *Till Death Us Do Part*. It is much more sanitized, and Archie, while a bigot, is shown as a much more easygoing and friendly figure. All of the characters in the American version are diluted, and in this respect they mirror something of considerable consequence.

In an egalitarian country like America, there is an immense and subtle pressure exerted upon people to conform, to be ordinary, to be "nice guys," and in consequence we find that the modal American personality lacks what might be called definition. The parameters are very narrow, and anyone who dares to develop a strong personality and identity risks being considered deviant, strange, and un-American, somehow. For to be an American is to be ab-

sorbed in the great anonymity of this country, to be like everyone else, to have an anonymous personality. Archie (*arch* is defined in the dictionary as "extreme, most fully embodying the qualities of his or its kind"; *bunker,* "full of bunk, nonsense") does not really have an individuated self. He is merely a strange combination of "nice-guy and bigot," but though he is a study in contradiction in qualities, there is nothing much else there. He is a personification of an abstraction—the law of contradiction.

Somebody has said that men adopt ideologies to shield themselves from the painful fact that their lives are minor events in the ongoing universe. But to grasp an ideology requires a certain kind of consciousness, and this seems to be beyond Archie Bunker's capacity. He is a pipsqueak with petty hatreds and ignorant prejudices. He is the American common man.

## ★ the new prometheus

Musical command he shows now in several respects: he has developed an incomparable jazz phrasing, and his emotional range is quite striking. Compare, for example, the genuine nostalgia of his *Moonlight in Vermont,* the sophisticated edge of *The Lady is a Tramp,* and the dramatic performance he gives to *One More for the Road.* His diction is impeccable—clear, hard, articulating the lyrical notes at the ends of lines or in the bridges on songs. The voice is now deeper, rougher, more sophisticated and dry than in the days when he was "momma's little boy" on the *Hit Parade*—but also much more interesting . . .

—STUART HALL
and PADDY WHANNEL,
*The Popular Arts*

I have chosen to deal with Frank Sinatra's "Spectacular" of Sunday, October 13, 1974, because it epitomizes some of the cultural dynamics found in this kind of program. Sometimes appearances such as this are called "specials" and sometimes "spectaculars," but whatever they are called, they represent something different—a rare appearance by a superstar into the humdrum world of everyday television, a semidivine intervention by a media demigod into the dreary wasteland of ordinary television.

The program was highly publicized with a full-page spread in the *San Francisco Examiner and Chronicle's* "Datebook" (entertainment magazine section). It showed Sinatra, his hands clasped above his head, as if he had just won the heavyweight championship of the world. The copy was simple: It announced, in enormous letters:

**S I N A T R A**
**The main event**
*live*

Both the title and the symbolism all suggested a championship bout—and for this dramatic "main event," Sinatra engaged the sports staff of ABC, so that everything would go perfectly.

As a review of the program by Sally Quinn of *The Washington Post* put it:

> The American Broadcasting Company claimed it was the first time in ten years that a major star had been televised live, in concert. Sinatra had chosen Roone Arledge, head of ABC Sports, as producer of the show—"The Main Event—Madison Square Garden."
>
> Sinatra felt nobody could produce a live broadcast better than ABC Sports, according to ABC Sports. Timing

had to be split-second. Commercials had to come at the right moment. And the show had to open and close so as not to waste a moment of precious air time, which was paid for by Ford Motor Company.

"I don't care how long you've been in this business," said 'the pope' during one of his unrehearsed commercial breaks, "there's nothing like a live audience." They went wild.

Unfortunately for Sinatra, who has now reached that pinnacle in which he is identified (like Einstein, for instance) by his last name alone, his program was only fortieth in the weekly ratings, a dismal failure. Everything was there—the technique of ABC, the press buildup, the ecstatic audience, the celebrities in the audience—but the "event" didn't quite come off and was not a great success, in part because Sinatra cannot sing very well anymore. It was a main event that had great significance for the social historian, and it is to the cultural implications of this program that I would like to turn.

It was called *The Main Event,* but who or what was Sinatra fighting? What was he the champion of? Who did he defeat? And what were the people in Madison Square Garden and across America getting out of the event?

On a very general level, Sinatra's audience was there to "participate in history," a gratification that explains a great deal of collective behavior. To nobodies, to anonymous personalities, to "little" people, nameless, faceless, obscure souls, attending the so-called concert (or doing so via the television program) gave them a place in history. They were there! And they were there along with the media celebrities, who lend an aura of glamour and occasion to each other's events. The world of entertainment

is incestuous, and performers do a great deal to keep one another before the public eye. The entertainment world is also beginning to resemble a hereditary aristocracy, as sons and daughters and nephews and nieces of movie stars and celebrities go into the field. In this respect Frank Sinatra is a great patriarch, having given the world a number of other lesser stars—his son Frank Sinatra Jr., his daughter Nancy, and so forth.

Thus his audience was more concerned with being there than with his singing. As the Sally Quinn article reports:

> As the audience filed out of Madison Square Garden, one disgruntled man said to his wife, "I thought he was terrible." "Terrible, schmerrible," she said. "He was Frank Sinatra."

The common man feels that being in the presence of greatness is, somehow, spiritually elevating and rewarding, and it was his presence rather than his presentation that counted.

Although the people who thought up the title *The Main Event* probably didn't recognize what they were doing, there are subtle implications in the title that have to do with the passing of time and ageing, and it might be asserted that one of the battles Sinatra was fighting was with Father Time. *The Main Event* was not really a concert; it was a play, a performance in which an authentic American heroic figure battled with the gods, affirming his identity and sense of himself in the face of tragic inevitability, asserting his personality and right to be unique against the blind forces of time and death, which rob all of us of these prized possessions.

So what if Sinatra has a monumental ego? So what if he hires mobsters and goons to shove people around? So what if he tells ethnic jokes and insults people. At least—and this is what is critical—he has an identity, he is *somebody!* In fact, and this is the source of his power, he insists upon the primacy of his personality and his right to be "Sinatra." He insists upon his right to be himself in spite of the powerful forces of conformity and depersonalization operating in American society. In this respect he is not different from many figures in the public eye, except that Sinatra is a complicated one and far more complex than the ordinary run-of-the-mill superstar.

Let me explain. In asserting the importance of will he affirms and reasserts a fundamental principal in the American mind—that a person's efforts and capacity for hard work are more important than the circumstances of his birth. During the broadcast he mentioned how he "took a four-cent ferry ride across the Hudson River to New York," and from his humble, Italian-American immigrant roots came a man who was to have his name splashed across the marquee of Madison Square Garden. It is the great Horatio Alger success myth—the nobody who becomes a somebody, the anonymous soul who becomes one of the four or five most identifiable figures in contemporary American society.

Thus, when Sinatra sang what he brazenly called "the national anthem," namely his current theme song "My Way," there was as much truth to the statement as megalomania. A look at this song reveals a number of things I've been talking about explicitly.

The themes of man's heroic battle against the forces of time and of the importance of being true to one's self

are the subject of this song. The phrases "end is near" and "final curtain" refer, immediately, to the end of a singer's act—but also imply the end of life. At this critical turning point, the hero states his "case," a case that he is certain to be true—and that is, in the final analysis, that nothing is important except being true to yourself.

And that is the genius of Frank Sinatra—the man who "dares" to be himself, to reveal his true feelings regardless of the consequences, to strip away the veneer of gentility and geniality that pervades our society and daringly expose himself. This is a traditional American point of view, more honored in the breach than practiced, however. In Sinatra's case, his willfulness has led to a loss of contact with reality, perhaps, and an unrealistic perception of his place in the sun—but he is different from the average American only in terms of the degree of his illusions and the scale of his feeling of power and potency. He is, in fact, only a traditional American writ large, so to speak.

What Emerson wrote about Napoleon can be said of Sinatra, though we must be mindful of the real significance of our two characters:

> He is no saint . . . and he is no hero, in the high sense. The man in the street finds in him the qualities and powers of other men in the street. He finds him, like himself, by birth a citizen, who, by very intelligible merits, arrived at such a commanding position that he could indulge all those tastes which the common man possesses but is obliged to conceal and deny: good society, good books, fast travelling, dress, dinners, servants without number, personal weight, the execution of his ideas, the standing in the attitude of a benefactor to all perhaps about him . . . precisely what is agreeable to the heart of every man . . . this powerful man possessed.

The two characters are different but they function for the

masses in a similar way. To return to Emerson:

> Bonaparte was the idol of the common men because he had
> in transcendent degree the qualities and powers of com-
> mon men.

The common man looks at Sinatra and sees himself, writ
large, and Sinatra's fights and disastrous marriages and es-
capades with the press are, in the common man's mind, his
experiences, his fights. Sinatra, in this respect, is only the
*instrument* of the common man's and woman's participa-
tion hunger, of his or her voracious need to be somebody,
to be known, to be loved, to be counted. What Sinatra does
not realize is that he is, in a sense, the creation of his audience, he is a puppet manipulated by his millions of adoring
fans. Sinatra thinks he does things his way, but this is illusion. He is not a hypocrite for he really believes in himself;
he is, it turns out, deluded. And that is the cruelest irony
of his situation; like Charlie McCarthy or any of the other
puppets, he does not recognize the source of his power and
the nature of his being.

At the concert women shrieked "I love you," and hys-
terical females crowded about trying to *touch* him, as if
contact with his body would have some kind of beneficial
and sacred significance. But the hysteria of the masses at
Madison Square Garden was really a kind of ego-squeak-
ing, in which nobodies lavished affection upon what they
must have subconsciously recognized to be the case—they
were saluting *their* creation. And Sinatra's heroic suffering,
the strained notes, the scratchy voice—all were testimonials
to the heroic magnanimity of the masses who "created"
him.

Rex Reed's review of the program in *The New York
News* was scorching. Reed's conclusion, that Sinatra is no

longer a Tiffany solitaire but rather a "Woolworth rhinestone, only serves to confirm what I have been talking about. The worse Sinatra is the greater and more magnanimous his fans (and creators) feel. And the nastier he is to them—such as turning his back and walking out without even saying goodbye to his audience at the "main event,"—the more satisfying he is to them and the more he confirms them. They look at their creation and see that it is "good."

Sinatra has been an important figure in the entertainment world for a long time, so there is a historical dimension to his career that is important, and which lends weight to his appearances. He has become, in a sense, an institution, and many people feel nostalgic about him. And curiously enough, at each stage in his development, he has metamorphisized into a relatively defined figure—from "bones" and "the battler" to "the chairman of the board." But what is most interesting is that there is a split in Sinatra that people have often noticed but seldom explained.

In the Sally Quinn article, she notices this phenomenon:

> He was his usual contrast of extraordinary vulgarity and exquisite taste, a wine one minute, particularly graceful the next, playing the audience like nobody else could, pushing them just far enough and bringing them back in a state of rapture. One moment there would be a luscious rendition of "Angel Eyes." The next would find him launched into:
> "A funny thing happened in Australia. I made a mistake and got off the plane. You think we've got trouble with one Rona Barrett (Hollywood gossip reporter). They've got 20 in Australia and each one's uglier than the other. Congress should give Rona Barrett's husband a medal for waking up beside her and having to look at her."

Not only does Sinatra play many roles and have many in-

carnations, but there seems to be a basic division within his personality. He wants to be taken seriously and strives for dignity, but he associates with gangsters and bums and frequently acts like a tramp. He is tough one moment, tender the next; mean and kind—a bundle of contradictions. Sinatra does not seem to have an integrated and unified personality, but is torn between conflicting pressures that toss him first one way, then another.

Sinatra's followers, who have created him in their image (if my assessment is correct), do not, then, have a hero who delivers all the goods, who presents a defined personality. He is not a fixed point as much as an oscillating one, but Sinatra's "split personality," "dissociated personality," or whatever we choose to call it, is only a mirror of the modal or typical American personality. Torn between conflicting ideals of achievement and Christian love, desires to "do our own things" and also for community, the typical American finds himself divided and suffering from a state of diffuse anxiety. He does not have a confirmed identity, a vital center that maintains continuity through time. Instead, like Sinatra, he appears in new roles from time to time—for he cannot resolve the internal contradictions in our culture and his personality. He can only act them out.

In the concluding chapter of *The Neurotic Personality of Our Time,* the distinguished psychoanalyst Karen Horney deals with some of these conflicts, which I have mentioned above. This chapter, entitled "Culture and Neurosis," argued that American culture was based on contradictions, which facilitated anxiety and frequently led to neurotic anxiety in this country. She suggested that there are three basic contradictory thrusts in American cul-

ture: First between "competition and success on the one hand, and brotherly love and humility on the other." Second, there is a contradiction "between the alleged freedom of the individual and all his factual limitations." This leads, she adds, to individuals "wavering between a feeling of boundless power in determining his own fate and a feeling of entire helplessness." There is also a contradiction between the overstimulation of our needs, by advertising and related institutions, and the limited possibilities we have of satisfying these needs. The discrepancy between our desires and what we can do about fulfilling them leads to frustration—and perhaps to a sense of worthlessness.

She concludes this chapter with a discussion of the contradictions in our culture, which I am presenting diagrammatically:

### CONTRADICTIONS IN AMERICAN CULTURE

| | |
|---|---|
| aggressiveness | yielding |
| excessive demands | fear of never getting anything |
| striving toward self-aggrandizement | feeling of personal helplessness |

Normal people, she adds, can generally cope with these contradictory tendencies but neurotic people cannot. These people who suffer from "culturally determined difficulties in an accentuated form, mostly through the medium of childhood experiences" are what she calls stepchildren of our culture. The dilemma we face in dealing with the destructive aspects of American culture and character, and with Sinatra as a manifestation of these phenomena, is that we cannot be certain where the blame lies. Where does our responsibility end?

I cannot answer this question but I can suggest an answer, and I will do this by returning to Emerson's essay on Napoleon. He ends his assessment of Napoleon by asserting that the Napoleonic experiment came to nothing and all of his heroic and destructive efforts ended with France "smaller, poorer, [and] feebler than he found it." He explains this as follows:

> It was the nature of things, the eternal law of man and of the world which baulked him and ruined him; and the result in a million experiments will be the same. Every experiment, by multitudes or by individuals, that has a sensual and selfish aim, will fail. . . . As long as our civilization is essentially one of property, of fences, of exclusiveness, it will be mocked by delusions. Our riches will leave us sick; there will be bitterness in our laughter, and our wine will burn our mouth. Only that good profits which we can taste with all doors open and which serves all men.

To condemn Sinatra, to condemn the stepchild of a society that creates egomaniacs, "monsters," whatever you will, in its own image is to place the burden on the victim. Sinatra is our "new Prometheus," and we cannot absolve ourselves of responsibility for him.

## ★ a fairy tale of self-destruction

In November, 1967, the following programs were listed by the Home Testing Institute as the top 10 among adults 18–34:

1. *Saturday Movies*
2. *Friday Movies*
3. *Thursday Movies*
4. *Wednesday Movies*
5. *Mission Impossible*
6. *Tuesday Movies*
7. *Dean Martin*
8. *I Spy*
9. *Sunday Movies*
10. *High Chaparral*

—BARRY G. COLE,
*Television:* Selections from
*TV Guide Magazine*

*Mission Impossible* is a classic reflection of the American

mind and a superb portrait of how the typical American sees himself and the world. Its great popularity is due, in part, to the fact that it is superbly crafted and acted, but also because it reaches us, and speaks to us, in the most profound way.

First of all, *Mission Impossible* has identity. It has a very strong and well-delineated format—starting off with the tape-recorded message and ending with some kind of an escape in a motor vehicle, after the mission has been accomplished. We might even say that *Mission Impossible* is based upon a formula, and this formula, instead of boring us, actually pleases us, reassures us.

Who does not remember the countless bizarre places in which Phelps finds the tape recorder and who does not know that the message on this recorder self-destructs five seconds after Phelps has listened to it? The tape recorder is our introduction into the world of espionage, into a world where brilliant and unscrupulous men are locked into combat, the outcome of which (we are told) is of momentous concern. Spy stories always have a world-historical dimension since they involve battles between nations that are fighting for dominance and, in some cases, survival.

Let us listen to one message, from a story entitled "The Submarine." As Phelps starts the tape recorder he removes a photograph from a manila envelope. It is a picture of a man who seems to be in his late fifties; his face is hard and arrogant. He looks dangerous. After saying, "Good morning, Mr. Phelps," the taped voice tells him he is looking at someone named Kruger Schtelman, who has been imprisoned for the past twenty-five years for war crimes in the "East European Republic." Schtelman is to

be released in three days. He is the only man alive who knows where an enormous fund of money stolen by the Nazis in World War II is hidden and he will undoubtedly use this money to finance a neo-Nazi plot in Europe.

Jim's mission (and the team's, also) is to find out where the money is hidden before the neo-Nazi's do. He is told, as usual, that "the Secretary" (meaning the government) will not admit to knowing anything about the Mission Impossible team. The tape then self-destructs five seconds after the final "Good luck, Jim."

With that, the tape goes *poof* and we are launched into an adventure. This tape recording is typical of the classic *Mission Impossible* program. The setting is in some Eastern European country, ruled by oppressive and undemocratic regimes, in this case, a state called "East European Republic."

The story involves the *Mission Impossible* force capturing Schtelman before he is released and tricking him into revealing where he has hidden the money. We learn that during his twenty-five-year imprisonment he has been continually subjected to interrogation—and even torture—by the East European police, who are after the same information. But he cannot be broken, even though the police threaten to murder him. This information is given to us in a scene between Schtelman and a police colonel named Sardner, who is supposedly an expert in making prisoners talk. Sardner tells Schtelman he will be killed if he does not tell where the money is, but that if he does, he will be protected.

Schtelman replies that nothing can make him talk and even invited Sardner to sign a death warrant that he's been threatening Schtelman with.

The problem Phelps faces, then, is how to extract information from a man who cannot be broken. Phelps's solution—and one that we find often in *Mission Impossible*—is to deceive Schtelman.

The team kidnaps Schtelman in a very elaborate and clever manner. He is gassed; and when he wakes up, he finds himself in a submarine, full of S.S. men and German naval personnel. Actually, he is in a mock-up of a submarine, which is located in an abandoned building in the East European Republic, but he does not know this. The situation is tense because time is a vital factor. Will the team get the information from Schtelman before the police, who have launched an elaborate search, find them? The country is sealed off and the police are moving closer and closer to the building where Schtelman is being deceived.

He is led to believe that the submarine, which supposedly is taking him to freedom, has been hit and that he has little chance of survival. In one of the final scenes, just before the "recognition scene," Schtelman reveals where the money is hidden. He has also been led to think that the S.S. people believe he is a traitor and cracked, and as Schtelman and Phelps (who is disguised as the captain of the submarine) move toward the torpedo room, Schtelman frets about being accused of "cracking." The Captain (Phelps) tells Schtelman that he knows whether or not he disclosed the information and that should be enough for him. But it isn't. Schtelman insists upon giving the Captain the account number, but the Captain says he doesn't want it, replying that he is a seaman, not a politican. Phelps then helps Schtelman enter the escape hatch. As he starts pulling the door shut, Schtelman shouts, desperately, "Captain—take it, Captain—the number."

Phelps replies he is not interested, but Schtelman will not be quieted. He shouts, "My old S.S. number—77326—Do you hear, Captain? It's the account number. Zurich National Bank." He tears his shirt open to reveal the number tattooed on his body, and shouts again, "Double seven three two six. . . ."

The scene then cuts to Barney, who has been manipulating the false submarine, and who has a headset on. He is shown writing the numbers down on a pad, which he hands to an associate. The mission has been accomplished. All that remains is the getaway, which is easily taken care of.

In the final scene of the story, as the team speeds away, Sardner and his men have closed in on the submarine. The hatch of the mock-up submarine rises slowly and we see Schtelman's head, with an oxygen mask, appearing. He rips off his mask and a close-up shows a bewildered face, blinking in the daylight. He throws his mask across the room, his face reflecting his rage and fury. He says, "Congratulations, Sardner . . . after twenty-five years . . . you got the information out of me."

Sardner suddenly recognizes what has happened and breaks into laughter over the irony of the situation. This matter of irony is of great importance, for one of the basic themes of the series is that life is, ultimately, ironic. Men who cannot be broken willingly give their information away, because their vanity is even stronger than their will. It may even be that irony is the fundamental perspective of the American. In our egalitarian society (in terms of our official values, that is), we cannot really have tragedy—at least in the formal, Aristotelian sense of the word, for we have no great men who can tumble from the heights.

In such a situation we become our own worst enemies, so to speak, and outsmart ourselves. And Schtelman's history may teach us something about one of our fundamental beliefs: like Schtelman, the average American tends to place great faith in his willpower. But like Schtelman, also, we can be manipulated—so that our belief in our willpower can be used against us, by people who can appeal to our vanity or other factors that motivate us. The more secure we are with the illusion that we cannot be manipulated, the easier it is for clever people to deceive us. In two hours the *Mission Impossible* team was able to do what the East European police weren't able to do in twenty-five years. This was because Phelps and his friends understand the essential helplessness of men. There is a key that unlocks all locks, a way to "get at" all men and women; and it is because Phelps recognizes this that what might seem to be impossible becomes merely a difficult job.

The theme of "mission" is an old one in American culture. In Ralph Henry Gabriel's classic study, *The Course of American Democratic Thought,* the notion that America has a mission in the world is listed as one of the three fundamental strands of American thought, from earliest times to the present. (The other two keystones are individualism and the notion of fundamental law, that there are absolutes, and that morality, therefore, is not conditional.) These three tenets have undergone modification and evolution over the years, but they have dominated our thinking from our earliest days to the present.

Our belief in our mission suggests that not only can we serve as an example to the world but also we have direct responsibility (ultimately in the name of self-interest) for ensuring that democracy, as we interpet it, triumphs! Thus,

*Mission Impossible* can be connected with our historic sense of mission and with a kind of diffuse anxiety about foreign nations which pose a threat to us.

We fear we are being deceived or might possibly be deceived, and we know, from experience, how easy it is to deceive people. In fact, the themes of deception and illusion are central to the series. There is little violence and physical force used. It is not necessary, and even counterproductive. Why use force when people can be made to do what you want them to do? In fact, it is generally posited that people cannot be *made* to do anything by force. The genius of *Mission Impossible* is that it creates what might be called "false realities," and in these false realities the various villains and heroes play out their roles, frequently unaware of what is really going on.

Reality is a many-layered thing. And so often what seems to be real is only illusion. We can see it, but the characters cannot. They cannot because they will not; they feel so secure in their powers and inviolability that they are pawns in the hands of the group.

Espionage is a team effort, and our interest in spy stories suggests some kind of a faint recognition that the self-made man, the private eye, the loner, is no longer adequate for big problems. Of course detectives and cowboys and other superindividualists still are more popular than secret agents for the general public, but this might be explained as a desire to hang on to our old nineteenth-century hope in the creative capacity of the individual to shape his destiny. But think how trivial the detective stories are in contrast to spy stories, when the fate of the world is contingent on the successful completion of missions that are "impossible."

We find ourselves on the horns of a dilemma. Nothing is impossible for Americans, because we believe willpower is efficacious in overcoming all problems. If you *really* want to be rich, or if you *really* want to do something, you can, as long as you persevere. And yet, as the program shows, our belief that willpower renders us immune from manipulation is naive. A good organization can bend us to its will—and we are susceptible to all kinds of control—so that we can even be made to act against our own interests, as the Schtelman case shows. For what we must all realize is that we cannot be secure and certain about anything. Identity is malleable—and many of the stories on *Mission Impossible* involve switched identities, false identities, and that kind of thing. This is always shown by having characters remove rubber masks in the resolution scenes. Our sense experience cannot be trusted, and we are fooled more often than we suspect.

There are, also, brilliant and unscrupulous secret agents who are out to steal our secrets, ruin our friends, and sabotage our plans. All this is going on all the time, but we, the ordinary people, know nothing of it. It is only because *Mission Impossible* provides us a peephole into this world of espionage that we find out about it, and what we discover is that our darkest fantasies are true!

But we also have reason to feel secure, for the *Mission Impossible* team of technological wizards is there to defend us. There is frequently an implicit conflict between foreign training and what might be called "native American genius." Foreign agents and their ilk are products of espionage academies, and other formal institutions. You don't get that feeling from the people on the *Mission Impossible*

team, who are casual and easygoing, though they always produce, even under stress. Phelps is, after all, *Mr.* Phelps —a good citizen who does an occasional impossible task.

The ambience of the series is one of complete technological mastery and omnipotence. Barney, the technological black, is capable of creating any effect, solving any technological problem—and represents, I believe, an attempt to place a black actor in a position where intelligence and other virtues are noticeable. Yet he can also be looked upon as a countercliché, and as, in effect, a modernization of the old Negro stereotype—the janitor. Barney is a supertechnological janitor, and though he fiddles with elaborate technological gadgets, he still has a role as fixer and odd-job man. From time to time he has escaped this role, but he generally is a subordinate figure.

There is a fairy-tale aspect of the series in that there is a kind of magic and power that is taken for granted. The team is always able to infiltrate enemy countries; it can do anything and everything it wants with ease, except for the final problem or ultimate task. That requires planning and effort and, what is most important, ingenuity. All the technology and organization exist only so that basic human weaknesses can be exploited. Phelps and his cohorts exude a kind of grace, and have the capacity to accomplish things almost effortlessly, since they are aware of—and can control, ultimately—the source from which all actions spring, the human psyche.

Most of the characters have a kind of one dimensionality about themselves, which heightens the suspense. Many people have commented that the women are very cold; this was especially the case when Barbara Bain was in the program. But all the characters, except the victims, have an

incredible amount of self-control and direction; it is only the villains who can be affected and who are capable of feelings and change. And I believe it is with the victims— who are generally villains—that the American public identifies, not with Phelps and his colleagues.

Thus, the final irony of this fairy tale is that we identify with the villains, the only people who are not zombies and automatons. They are the only humanized figures (despite all the terrible things they may have done), and they are the only characters who are permitted to have a shock of recognition—even if this shock is frequently limited to the realization of having been "had." For when we see these poor duped fools, volunteering what could not be taken from them, acting against their own interests, victims of deception and self-deception, do we all not have a similar shock of recognition? Do we not have a fleeting recognition that the history of Schtelman and his brethren has been our history in certain important ways?

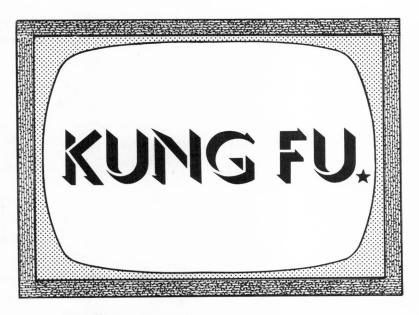

## ★ the resolution of the dialectic

Puritan fearfulness is best explained in terms of the actual experiences of exile, alienation, and social mobility about which the saints so often and insistently wrote. Discipline and repression are responses to these experiences, responses which do not aim at a return to some former security, but rather at a vigorous control and a narrowing of energies— a bold effort to shape a personality amidst "chaos."

—MICHAEL WALZER,
"Puritanism as a Revolutionary Ideology"

In the early seventies *Kung Fu* was a rage that seemed to pervade American culture. The program, starring David Carradine, was extremely popular; Kung Fu films, Kung Fu clubs, children playing Kung Fu were to be seen every-

where. Then, suddenly, it lost its hold on the American imagination and now the program wanders around its network, looking for a home and a place in the sun, much as Caine, its hero does.

America has always had a fascination with Eastern culture and there are devotees of the various Eastern martial arts, Indian gurus, Zen Buddhists, Sokka-Gakkai missionaries, and Chinese restaurants scattered across the length and breadth of the country. After former-president Richard Nixon's trip to China, during which television stations carried broadcasts from Peking and other Chinese cities by the hour, the country was engulfed by a wave of books, programs, and films with Chinese themes and topics.

Actually the program *Kung Fu* is a spin-off from the big rage for Kung Fu movies, which erupted out of Hong Kong and catapulted the late Bruce Lee to fame and the proverbial fortune before he died at the age of thirty-two. Lee made only four movies, but they became international hits and firmly established the genre. Some critics have suggested that *Kung Fu* (I will use italics to identify the television program and separate it from the genre) is something new, something different on the American cultural scene. After all, its hero is an oriental priest who is practiced in an Eastern martial art, and the pacifist ambience of the program also seems at first glance a bit unusual.

However, if you look at the program carefully you find that aside from these rather superficial traits, *Kung Fu* is as American as chop suey. Though Caine, the hero of *Kung Fu,* is an oriental priest, he is, nevertheless, half-American. He is the product of a union of a white American father and a Chinese mother, and in Caine we find a meeting of East and West and a *reconciliation of a dialectic that exists*

*in the American imagination* and which is echoed in the program. The structure of the program is that of a dialectic resolved, ultimately, in a ritual combat. But more about this shortly.

Caine, like all Americans, is a spiritual orphan—a man on a quest, looking for his roots, his "self." In search of this elusive self, and an outcast from a despotic China, he wanders through the wasteland of the American West. He finds, in the course of looking for a usable past, that he is unwittingly involved, at every turn, in other matters—so that his private quest takes on social dimensions; in trying to redeem himself he finds he must redeem society around him.

Frequently he finds himself defending racial minorities—Chinese, Mexicans, and others—against a bewildering assortment of villains. In each case he finds himself forced to act, forced to use his powers to save himself or his friends (or both) from antagonists who cannot understand the dimensions of his strength or the intensity of his commitment. In keeping with the American notion of what spirituality is like and with the clichés in the common mind about religious sensibility, Caine is portrayed as someone terribly solemn and glum. An English critic, Peter Lennon, commented about this in a review of the program that appeared in *The Sunday Times*:

> On ITV we had *Kung Fu*, which was at least a painstaking attempt to launch a new cult figure: an American trained in the Chinese art of self-defense. A pacifist killer in good causes. The opening episode was elaborately worked out; good photography, sequences well edited and thrills spaced out with careful calculation.
>
> But *Kung Fu* is afflicted with a defect, which is com-

mon to a great many modern American television heroes: he is an unbearably glum creature. He is also sanctimonious. The mistake was to have not cast an oriental in the role; there the tactiturn quality would have had a sheen of mythical inscrutability. A crew-cut American with the fleshy face of a college soft-ball player, suggests only that he is suffering from postadolescent depression.

Caine is glum because in the American Protestant mind spirituality is glum and all the new American Christ figures walking around in the mid-seventies wallow about in a veneer of sentimental solemnity and glumness, demonstrating that they are playing roles and little else. People without a sense of tragedy can imagine no other options.

There is a strong and perhaps simplistic moralism about the series. Each adventure is meant to teach us a lesson about life, and this is made explicit by the flashback technique that is so dominant and, to my mind, beautifully used. In each tale the flashback permits the audience to see a second variation or reading of the episode, with Caine's master in the monastery explaining, in symbolic terms, the lesson to be learned. Something that took place in the Chinese monastery, where Caine was raised, always has meaning and is relevant to something taking place in any given episode.

In a recent adventure, we find Caine being taught by one of the monks, who is one of his masters. This master's family is murdered by the agents of the Emperor and the master barely escapes to America with the lone survivor of his family, a young nephew. Years later Caine meets the master and finds himself involved in a very difficult situation. It seems that the nephew of the master was killed by

being run over by a train, and the master—now partially deranged—is avenging himself by blowing up the railroad. Inadvertantly, Chinese railroad workers (who are shown being cruelly exploited by the railroad) are killed. Caine finds himself torn between two powerful forces: on the one hand there is the tradition, which has been bred into Caine in the monastery, of reverence and obedience owed to masters, and on the other hand there are the demands of social justice and morality.

The situation is resolved via ritual combat. Caine fights and defeats his Kung Fu master, who then (so we are to assume) wanders off, having learned his lesson. "No man," Caine tells the master, "is all powerful." Yes! "Power corrupts and absolute power corrupts absolutely," to paraphrase Lord Acton. It might be argued that the philosophizing in *Kung Fu* is simplistic and banal; this may be true. But my point is that this moralizing is very much in keeping with the American spirit—as is the theme of the reluctant hero, who only fights after he is attacked or when he is cornered.

*Kung Fu* plays upon our fantasies about power, and, in particular, about natural power, about power in our fists and body. We learn that this power is dangerous and must be kept under control, and are shown that the man who is powerful and knows he is powerful is the meek man, the mild man, the quiet man, the man who even goes out of his way to avoid trouble. He does not have to prove anything to other people—or himself—since he is secure in his identity.

In *Kung Fu* the combats usually have a ritualistic quality and are presented in a highly structured and formal-

ized manner. Much use is made of slow motion, which symbolizes the passage from ordinary time to a kind of timelessness—unconsciousness or even death. We are seldom sure which, for after the combat scenes, which are always concluded with an aura of finality, we quickly move on to other matters—usually Caine's departure. He has been tested and not found wanting, and now must resume his quest—the only battle he faces, which he cannot win, is this search for his origin and for his "lost" American roots.

I have, to this point, identified a number of themes and aspects of *Kung Fu* that relate it to American culture and American values. I have suggested that Caine is a "spiritual orphan" like many Americans (who are also immigrants), and that, like them, he finds himself on a quest. His mission inevitably involves him in fighting for justice and truth, frequently on the side of the underdogs and oppressed minorities. In keeping with the American popular imagination, as a man of God he is portrayed as a solemn, perhaps even glum, figure, since we equate spirituality and depth with solemnity. And, as is so often the case in American popular culture and the American imagination, he (as "youth") teaches older and more powerful figures (even one of his masters in the episode described) lessons about morality and justice.

I would like to turn from this subject to one I mentioned earlier, namely the dialectical structure of the program. In each program we generally find ourselves drawn between opposites, so that a kind of dialectical process is established, which is finally resolved at the end of each episode. To see this more clearly, examine the following chart:

## OPPOSITIONS IN *KUNG FU*

| China | America |
|---|---|
| emperor evil | common man evil |
| civilized East | wild West |
| history and civilization | nature |
| spiritual depth | spiritual shallowness |
| power in man (internal) | power in weapons (external) |
| the past (flashbacks) | the present |
| institutions (monastery) | discrete individuals |
| community | society |
| yellow | white |
| youth subservient: learns | youth dominant: teaches |
| confirmed identity | diffused identity |
| totalitarian society | anarchy |
| political subjugation | economic subjugation |

## RESOLUTIONS IN *KUNG FU*

Half-white, half-yellow, half-Chinese, half-American hero uses wisdom and powers from East to survive in West. Brings order and justice to anarchic society.

Although this chart represents something in the way of a simplification, I do believe it demonstrates, rather clearly, that there is a dialectic in the program; we are asked to reconcile opposites, and the success of the program is due to the fact that it accomplishes this in a satisfactory manner. I am not arguing that audiences are aware that these oppositions exist in their minds and in the American imagination, or that they are conscious of them. I do believe that they are affected by them since there is a fund-

amental dialectic in the American mind, which defines
America in contrast to Europe and also, now, the so-called
"inscrutable" East.

China is portrayed as a totalitarian and corrupt land
in which evil is incarnated in the Emperor. It is an
ancient and old civilization, but we find cruelty there
along with wisdom. The two dominant Chinese institutions, for our purposes, are the monastery where Caine is
raised, and the Court of the Emperor. America, on the
other hand, is a wilderness full of lawless despots, where
evil is incarnate in the common man and not necessarily a
small group of corrupt rulers. Evil can exist, then, anywhere—and just because a society has spiritual depth, like
China, doesn't mean it is any better. Indeed, we might
argue that the spiritual lightweights in America are ignorant and don't know any better; when they learn they are
capable of change.

Our view of China is confined, generally, to the monastery, where we find a community of saints and scholars
living in harmony and peace. The greatest of the masters
in the monastery is a blind man who is Caine's spiritual
father and who teaches him about life at the same time he
initiates him into the mysteries of Kung Fu. In this monastery there are rites, there are tasks, there is a path, and
everyone in the monastery has what might be called a "confirmed" identity. They know who they are and what they
are, except, that is, for Caine. He also has a secure identity,
but this is tarnished by the mystery of his origins, his roots
in America, and it is the search for this missing piece in
the puzzle of his identity that brings Caine to the American
West.

Caine finds himself in a moral wilderness of individ-

uals at war with one another and, of course, with themselves. They are a group of spiritual lightweights who need
teaching, and they recognize in Caine's calmness and, ultimately, in his power, that he has depth and much to teach
them. At the end of the episode dealing with the master
who dynamited the railroad, the railroad inspector (whose
job it was to find the dynamiter) leaves the railroad, after
securing better conditions for the Chinese workers. He can
no longer justify to his conscience working for the unscrupulous railroad owners who exploit the Chinese so
cruelly. America may not have cruel monarchs, monsters
with political power, but it has, instead, economic monarchs who tyrannize people as cruelly as political ones.

We find something rather interesting here—the recognition that evil can arise out of innocence as well as knowledge, it can arise in a wild and barbarous West as well as
an effete and overcivilized East. In America, however, the
evildoers are out of their class when they get into a fight
with Caine, and they tumble through the air in dazzling
slow-motion with a look of incredulity and awe. The brut-
ish barbarians of the Wild West are like children in the
hands of this quiet Kung Fu master, who unites in himself
the moral fervor of the Protestant West and the technique
of the East.

The price Caine pays for his power is celibacy! Few
can make such a sacrifice, but in this respect he is not un-
like many of the gunslingers in the westerns who also renounced love for power and a different kind of potency.
One thinks of Shane, for example, as a similar kind of
figure—a wanderer who appears, fights an incarnation of
evil, and rides off into the mountains. Heroes like Caine
cannot marry the schoolmarm; their love is of a higher

order. In truth it is a modern manifestation of ascetic Protestantism, which dominates to this day, in many respects, American culture and the American imagination. The essential purity of Caine, his dedication, his unswerving devotion to his cause—all have the flavor of an undiluted Puritanism, masked in the guise of an oriental monk with strange powers.

I cannot leave this analysis of *Kung Fu* without saying something about the technical qualities of the program. Generally speaking it is beautifully done, and the photography is frequently brilliant, capturing and conveying an aura of mystery and magic. The use of the flashbacks contribute to this; time is interrupted and we move backwards and forwards through it at various speeds. The way time is used tells us that things as well as people are not always as they seem, and one cannot count on everything proceeding forward on a regular basis. These flashbacks also reflect that the program is based on a very sophisticated understanding of how our minds work, for it does not proceed forward all the time but, rather, mirrors the "stream of consciousness" in our minds. Our minds race back and forth through time, from memories of the past to speculations about the future, and the program does the same thing.

Caine is a quintessential American hero—one more spiritual orphan wandering about through the American moral wilderness in search of personal salvation and achieving it, like most of our heroes, through the redemption of his fellowman.

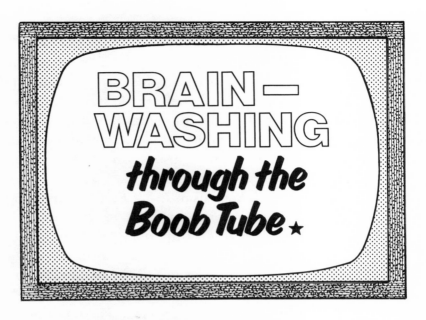

BRAIN—
WASHING
*through the
Boob Tube* ★

★ **the cultural significance of two commercials***

It is estimated that by the time the average child reaches the age of sixteen, he will have viewed more than 640,000 commercials. (This figure was mentioned by California State Senator George Moscone in hearings on food advertisements and children held in California recently.) If we assume that each commercial lasts an average of thirty seconds, it would mean the child spends approximately 5,300 hours watching commercials or the equivalent of three working years. That is, if a person had a job watching commercials alone, it would take him three years of work at eight hours a day to watch his allotment, up to age six-

* Adopted from Arthur Asa Berger, *Pop Culture*, (Pflaum/Standard).

teen. Quite obviously the amount of time devoted to the program content is even more astronomical.

Generally speaking we do not pay much attention to the cultural significance or social consequences of commercials. We see them as minor irritants, the "price we have to pay" for our "free" television. I think it is naive to dismiss commercials as trivial or innocent because any given one is seldom more than thirty seconds long. *When you total up the amount of exposure each person has the figures are staggering.* If we think of commercials as expensive, skillfully made "playlets," and works of art meant to shape our behavior and using every device available to this end, then commercials become a subject of considerable interest.

I would now like to explore, briefly, some of the cultural meanings in two commercials—one for Levis and the second for McDonald's hamburgers. I am using each commercial as a *signifier* and am dealing with what is *signified* by the commercial. If commercials are to be functional they must relate to cultural problems and cultural imperatives, so that an analysis of commercials is a useful way at getting at the values and beliefs in the society where the commercials are broadcast.

### "The Stranger from the House (Tribe) of Levi"

One reason this advertisement attracted my attention is because I happen to know the copywriter who dreamed it up. He told me that he has absolute freedom and the company does not restrict him in any way, which is something rather unusual. Most advertising agencies work under rather stringent restrictions and have to satisfy their customers, who are often conservative and unimaginative. In

addition to the restrictions imposed on agencies by the companies, at times networks also cause problems. The point is, then, that most copywriters work within rather tight boundaries. Such is not the case with Levis.

"The Stranger," which is the title of the mini-drama, involves a mysterious figure who suddenly appears in a town where people seem to be colorless, and leading lives of presumably quiet desperation. The Stranger brings people Levis, which adds color to their lives (and style) and then wanders off, in search of new triumphs. We sense, from the mystical and dramatic quality of the commercial, that there is something remarkable about this person. He has a sense of mission and something perhaps "divine" about him. Certainly, his "identity," that of being a stranger, is quite suggestive.

What this commercial represents is a fusion of two themes—*the lonesome cowboy* (perhaps gunfighter) who "cleans up" a town being dominated by crooks, and *the Christ figure,* who possesses mysterious powers. Both figures actually have an evangelical quality; their mission is redemption of fallen man. The Stranger is bringing "good news," namely that Levis are colorful, in stripes and patterns, and have interesting textures. Levis are not just blue jeans.

After he has magically transformed the people of the town he leaves and disappears as suddenly as he appeared. The voice of the announcer is unctuous and properly so, for we have watched a dramatization of a parable. In modern terms it might be described as follows: "How the mysterious Christ-Cowboy stranger turned the drab town folk onto jazzy threads." I might point out here that I think this commercial is, in terms of its mission, brilliant; it is fascin-

ating, beautifully realized, and remarkable. It is a satiri-
zation of the cowboy and Christ tale, yet it has just enough
dramatic integrity so as to be taken seriously, also. It is a
double joke on us—a "put on" telling us what to put on!

But it is not, if you think about it, very reassuring. We
are given a picture of the general public in a rather bad
way. They are listless, colorless, drab, dull, boring, and un-
exciting. It is only through the intervention of a super-
natural (?) mysterious figure that they are able to snap out
of their doldrums. And all it takes is a pair of pants! Being
dependent upon mysterious strangers is not a happy state
of affairs, as anyone who has read Mark Twain's *Mysterious
Stranger* knows.

It is a rather amusing, and perhaps mysterious, coincidence that the House of Levi has taken on the function
of the Tribe of Levi—for they are the priests (both of them)
concerned in various ways with men's salvation and redemption. I happened to see this commercial while I was
watching *The Immortal,* the story of a man relentlessly
pursued by forces, which have every technological contri-
vance at their disposal. Between the two of them, the program and the commercial, we find dramatic presentation of
a number of themes plaguing modern man: the sense of
being pursued by mysterious forces, the sense of being
powerless (especially when compared with mysterious
strangers), feelings of boredom, anxiety, and so forth. Plac-
ing the commercial in *The Immortal* was perfectly logical,
since they complement one another perfectly.

The title of the commercial, "The Stranger," has
other social and political implications. Strangers exist
where there is no community, no bonds between people.
Indeed, just the opposite is usually the case: self-interest

and the quest for personal advantage make everyone an enemy or a potential one, since his interests may conflict with ours. "The Stranger" in this advertisement is a producer, figuratively and symbolically, and the people are consumers, and those seem to be the only relationships of any significance. The relationship of advertising and "producer-consumer roles, has been explored by Stuart Hall and Paddy Whannel in *The Popular Arts* (p. 317):

> . . . since the producer is autonomous, with the means of production at his disposal, making decisions about production as it affects the profitability of his business, and the consumer is assumed to be the private individual making personal choices about the consumption of goods, advertising must legitimize the market relationship and define society in terms of its commanding images. Implicit in advertising as a communication process, then, is the alienation of the sphere of work from the sphere of consumption. Advertising sees us as individual consumers making private decisions at the expense of others in the universal supermarket, the great bazaar; it cannot see us as users of a common stock of produced goods and services which we both help to create and, in our turn, need. In these terms, advertising is an extension of the market system and can be legitimately described as the official art of a capitalist society.
>
> A market which is organized by this kind of art has the advantage of leaving open a wide range of choices. But it has the disadvantage of highlighting the personal as against the social, consumption of goods and services. It defines all needs in terms of personal consumption, though it is clear that many of the real and pressing social decisions in our society cannot be adequately taken in this way. . . . One of the charges against advertising is that, by investing only those choices which we make as private individuals with the glamour of art, it depresses in the public

consciousness major areas of life where social decisions are urgent.

In this respect, advertising reinforces and reflects certain fundamental traits in our society, such as individualism and privatism* (the neglect of social concerns). Thus, the final irony—"The Stranger" has been amongst other strangers, who, in a sense, must always remain strangers unto one another.

In the commercial, the role of "The Stranger" is somewhat unclear—he brings clothes full of color and vitality to people who are dull and drab, but does he *sell* them the clothes? The mysticism and pseudoreligiosity of the ad evade this question. The merchandiser becomes God-like, a kind of divinity, but he is not preaching a social gospel by any means. In fact, it is implicitly an antisocial gospel.

It may seem that I am persecuting this poor "Stranger," and making some kind of a monster out of a saintly fellow trying to make people aware of Levis. I may be overemphasizing certain things in the interest of calling our attention to certain psychological themes and socio-political implications that stem from these themes—but this is necessary because we are exploring new territory, so to speak. *Images are resonant, and have vibrations (cultural meanings) of great amplitude.* These "vibrations" may not be obvious, but they are there. People may not be fully conscious of what is happening to them when they see a commercial such as "The Stranger," but I believe something is happening, which may be affecting and speaking to their subconscious states, and, in turn, influencing their actions.

* In The *New Industrial State* J. K. Galbraith argues that advertising has replaced Puritanism as a means of motivating people to work. We work so we can consume, not to show our love of God.

It is images that trigger our actions; not rational appeals, but emotional ones. We must remember that the function of advertising is not to inform but to persuade and this is facilitated by emotional appeals, not rational ones.

### "The Millionaire Who Loves McDonald's Hamburgers"

This advertisement is a remarkable one which utilizes a kind of reverse snob-appeal for McDonald's hamburgers, a popular chain of fast-food stands with quick service, a limited menu, and inexpensive prices. I have always been interested in McDonald's (and other fast-food emporiums) as a cultural phenomenon of considerable importance, and their millionaire hamburger eater is, in himself, a compelling cultural image with all kinds of implications.

We see a uniformed servant in a Rolls Royce transporting a silver tray of impressive size. It is covered and we have no idea what is in it, or what product is being advertised. He stops in front of a mansion, and carries the tray through great columns and down long corridors. Finally, he enters a huge room at which sits a man in a luxurious dressing gown. Everything to this point is connected with luxury, wealth, elite tastes, and that kind of thing. The servant is obviously as snobbish as his employer, who sits, alone, at a large and ornate table.

The servant brings the beautiful tray to the man, takes off the cover, and on it we see some McDonald's hamburgers, French fries, and a milk shake. The servant stands at attention. The millionaire's face lights up when he sees the hamburgers and other goodies from McDonald's. Then he looks sternly at the servant, who hesitates for a moment and then, embarrassed, gives the millionaire his change.

The point is, we are told, that you can get hamburgers, French fries, and a malt from McDonald's for less than a buck. And the millionaire knows this as well as his servant. The image of the millionaire showing delight when he sees the hamburgers has also been used in magazine advertisements. It is, in essence, humorous. There is something strange about a rich and powerful man being delighted by something as common and cheap as a lowly McDonald's hamburger. It is quite incongruous, and we are shocked when we discover what it is that has delighted this man—and what was under the cover of that fancy tray.

There is a good deal of suspense generated by the first part of the commercial, which is silent. This heightens the humor. On the other hand, the image of the rich man indulging in the pleasures of the common man has a comforting aspect. Almost anyone can afford a McDonald's hamburger, so at least some of the good things in life *are* available to all. The incongruity of having a rich man eat a common man's food is implicitly a reaffirmation of our basic equalitarianism and democratic nature, despite all the trappings of wealth and exclusiveness in the commercial. "Don't you see," it says "the rich aren't that much different from the man on the street, except they have more money. *They* don't think they are better than you are, otherwise, why would they be eating McDonald's hamburgers?"

Of course the millionaire is not eating his hamburger in a parking lot or on one of McDonald's tables, but that is not the important thing. What is significant is that he is showing that he is an ordinary guy, who likes a good hamburger!

None of the above is explicit, but for the commercial to work there must be a number of common beliefs and

attitudes in the minds of most people about all the things I've been talking about. I would even speculate that the creators of the ad probably didn't consider all its social and political implications, as far as class relations are concerned. This is because a rich millionaire eating McDonald's hamburgers (and that sort of thing) is all part of the general fund of ideas of conventional wisdom of the popular mind, and is so much a part of us that we don't even think twice about it. We tend to see ourselves as a classless middle-class people, though this notion may be ending with the rise of radicalism in the universities and with the impact of radical ideas on American thought in general. *Our equal access to McDonald's, then, becomes the proof of the pudding of our great democratic society.*

The whole franchise industry, of which McDonald's is a most successful example, has been interpreted as "significantly" American. These franchises represent the last frontier, so to speak, in merchandising—the last chance for the little man to own a business of his own. Unfortunately, so many franchises have been established and the competition has been so great, that large numbers of them fail, leaving the people who bought them with little to show for their investments—but that is a matter tangential to our concerns, though, in a sense, the McDonald's commercial may ironically be relevant here.

After all, it is the wish of many Americans to be rich. The peculiar nature of American society, with its alleged open mobility (supposedly uniquely American and often tied to "The American Dream") facilitates this, so that the common man, at least so the theory goes, opens his franchise and becomes a millionaire, if everything works out perfectly. Granted there is a great deal of hard work, but

we all know that "where there is a will there is a way." Perhaps, to continue with this story, he becomes a millionaire and is able to seat himself at a fancy table in luxurious clothes and wait for the butler to bring him dinner. What does he get when he lifts the silver cover on the tray? A hamburger! Was it worth it? Has he been gypped? This little story carries the irony in the millionaire who loves McDonald's hamburgers to a fanciful and absurd conclusion, but though stated in an extreme way, it is a question that a large number of Americans are asking themselves.

So much for the analysis of a couple of culturally interesting commercials. There are many commercials, which have little cultural baggage or resonance, and others which, like the two I've discussed, have a great deal that is significant in them. *Anacin* ads, for example, are generally irritating combinations of everyday and common events (truck drivers with headaches) and mystery stories ("with more of the ingredient that doctors recommend most"). Laura Scudder commercials for *Taco Chips* show a *homunculus,* in whose hands regular size chips look gigantic. *Saab* automobiles talks about "well-built Swedes," but they mean automobiles, not women. I might go on and on but I think I have made my point, namely that commercials are interesting and are full of significant images and socio-cultural materials. It is quite possible that they have a powerful socializing effect and may be providing an education, libidinal and not liberal, which we should concern ourselves with a bit more.

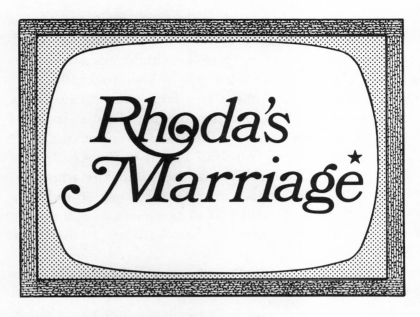

## ★ plain Janes have less pains

It shapes up as the biggest social event of the new TV season. On Oct. 28, a Bronx window dresser named Rhoda Morgenstern married a building wrecker named Joe Girard before 20 million viewers. Rhoda's old pals from "The Mary Tyler Moore Show" are also in attendance—and very much in character.

—NEWSWEEK,
Oct. 7, 1974

The marriage of Rhoda Morgenstern to Joe Girard was one of the television events of the last week of October, 1974. The program was quite popular—coming in tenth in the Nielsen ratings—and attracted a great deal of coverage in the print media. Even the sports commentators on

the *Monday Night Football* games, on a different channel, talked about it. It was, as one television critic described it, "a blockbuster." In honor of the occasion the program was given a full hour—a conventional sign of importance. Since time is money on television (and elsewhere, too, many tell us), a program one hour long automatically takes on much more status and dignity. Expanding the program to one hour for this episode thus turned it into a media "event."

Unfortunately it was not a terribly satisfactory event, though it was not a disaster. The episode revolved around one of the most difficult and trying ceremonies in our culture—a wedding. Since this wedding involved Jews and took place in New York, we all could be assured of a great deal of chaos as colorful characters paraded on and off the stage of life.

Weddings, we all know, are social events that are held and controlled by the parents of the bride; and in this episode we found that although Rhoda and Joe wanted a small intimate marriage, Rhoda's mother, a formidable female and a classic Jewish mother, wanted a big wedding—and she got her way. No illusions are going to be fostered on *Rhoda*; the program, it is suggested, is going to tell it like it is. And the truth of the matter is that weddings *are* for parents; Rhoda and Joe are not autonomous, and their wishes are important but not critical. It is a fitting irony that marriage is a rite of passage in which the leading actors celebrate their release from bondage and control by parents in a ceremony controlled by the parents.

And it is Rhoda's task to reveal that such is the case. The situation has changed from what it was in the *Mary Tyler Moore show*. In that program the basic situation was that of courtship, and there was even a flashback in Rhoda's

marriage program to those not really very happy days. An assortment of bizarre men was paraded out—various kinds of kooks and weirdos that Rhoda and Mary were involved with. It was all funny, but also rather sad. That is one of the truths we get from *Mary Tyler Moore*, a never-ending, antisentimental kind of soap opera, whose basic ploy is honesty, and the recognition of man's and woman's capacity for being slightly mad . . . or strenuously neurotic.

Both *Mary Tyler Moore* and *Rhoda* capitalize on this antisentimental tell-it-like-it-is stance. In one scene during the marriage episode, Rhoda confesses to Joe that she is difficult to live with, that she has eating fantasies, that in personal relationships she either attacks or withdraws, and that she has hang-ups about her mother. Honesty is the policy for Rhoda. Joe, in turn, admits that he has problems, too—*even* that he has wondered whether he is taking the right step. Yes, indeed—the truth shall set you free.

And yet *Rhoda* is based on one of the most common bits of conventional wisdom in the American popular mind —that plain girls get married more easily than beautiful ones. Poor Mary. She is beautiful, she is kind, she is intelligent, she has personality, but she is thirty-four and not married. Of course she cannot get married because the controlling conception in the program is that of the adventures a single woman has in making her way in the real world. Notice, however, that the central focus is on dating and romance, as if that aspect of a woman's life is the only one that really counts.

Plain girls get married more easily than beautiful ones because, for one thing, men are afraid of beautiful women, and for another, beautiful women don't need to get married to enjoy life. Marriage, in the public mind (and in the pop

culture world) is debilitating, though there are lots of comic possibilities in the plain Jane's search-for-love theme.

But it is not so much the destructive aspects of marriage that scare men away from beautiful women; rather it is the threat they pose to men's egos. There is the threat of competition from others and by implication, the "performance" problem. Beautiful women activate repressed anxieties and return men to adolescence, when they had to fight for women against bigger and more powerful figures, such as their brothers and fathers and older friends. Inevitably, also, the matter of sexual potency becomes critical. Can the man who is married to the beautiful woman satisfy her? Can he keep her?

In additon, beautiful women activate infantile anxieties, for the beautiful woman becomes in strange ways the idealized picture of their (beautiful) mother that men carry around in their heads. Thus, there is an implicitly incestual component involved in loving and being loved by a beautiful woman—and lurking in the background is a fear of punishment and ultimately castration. This castration can take the form of a fear of the actual punishment, or can be symbolic and manifest itself in impotence.

These problems are usually exacerbated by the beautiful female, who has learned to expect attention and who usually suffers from too much self-love. Various consequences occur. As Dr. Milton Sapirstein explains this phenomenon in his book, *Paradoxes of Everyday Life,* the paradox of the beautiful woman is that

> . . . her relations with the opposite sex are never casual, never easy. Other girls have friendships with boys which may, or may not, ripen into romance. They have time to get acquainted, to explore each other's feelings and atti-

tudes, to decide what they mean to one another. The young beauty is "rushed" from the beginning. Boys want to make love to her at sight and very soon do.

Under attack all the time, the beautiful girl rallies her defenses, but at great cost:

So she rebuffs the boys vigorously, putting a break on her own feelings in the process and perhaps, in her anxiety, repressing them altogether. She is still waging a defensive war on two fronts but one of them is now unconscious. That furious battle in the depths of her personality lays waste her energies. Later, when she wants to, she cannot "recall" her sexual impulses. She has become frigid.

Although he is not writing about the *Mary Tyler Moore* show, Sapirstein's description of the difficulties the beautiful woman has in her relationships with males convinces me that the genius of the program is that it is an evocation of the dilemma of the beautiful woman that is remarkably accurate, psychoanalytically speaking.

For circling around the beautiful woman—and Mary —are a collection of men whom Sapirstein describes as unsatisfactory in various ways. There are wolves whose only interest is sexual conquest; there are neurotic inadequate types; there are sadists and all kinds of other figures. In the program we do not get any figures who are pathological or dangerous, but the dynamics of the problem of the beautiful woman are revealed.

What happens in the program, in essence, is that this situation—of great importance to our psyches in ways that we are unaware of—is turned into a travesty of sorts, distorted and milked for laughs. But enough of the situation comes through to us so that behind the comedy we find a

kind of sustenance and can work through some of the problems we face.

Mary can never marry, for if she does the psychological dynamics activated by the program will be sacrificed. Rhoda Morgenstern, her less attractive friend, must be married.

I suspect Rhoda was married off also because MTM Productions (which has a number of situation comedies in its stable) doesn't want to have two competing programs. Thus *Rhoda* was turned into a domestic comedy—one of the stables of the situation comedy format. But it claims to be different in that it isn't absurd and silly, but honest. In the October 7, 1974, *Newsweek* article on the program, "*Rhoda*—A Star is Spun Off," we find the following description of the program (and of the philosophy of the company, MTM Productions, which produces it):

> MTM's trademark is the humane humor that flows from recognizable characters rather than contrived situations. You don't have to be Jewish to love Rhoda; she's the slightly dippy single who lives down everyone's block, the one who didn't get up the gumption to leave the family apartment until she was 24. "My mother," Rhoda ruefully confides, "still refers to this as the time I ran away from home." Her frumpy younger sister has inherited all of Rhoda's neuroses. When not noshing on beef potpies, Brenda frets about sex ("I'm still getting over the what-fun-to-be-a-woman hoax") and dates losers like Lenny, whose idea of lovemaking is to suggest "Let's touch our toes."

Yet the marriage episode involved a rather enormous suspension of disbelief. For the episode hinged on Rhoda being late for her own marriage because she waited for

hours for a ride from a person she detested and who is defined as a self-centered lame-brain. It was further posited that she could not even catch a cab. Thus she takes the subway, all decked out in her bridal costume, and arrives several hours late for her wedding.

Is that not a contrived situation? And are not the mother and father and most of the other characters clichés or counterclichés? The program is antisentimental with vengeance, but that does not mean it is realistic. I do not think it is particularly realistic to have a world made up of losers and neurotics. There may be many of both in the world, but they are not always funny and it is not necessarily humane to present them as objects of ridicule.

This program, and all situation comedies (sitcoms), lead us to an interesting question. Is individualism, as we know it, disappearing from the American scene—or changing in fundamental ways? In 1974 there were 15 sitcoms on network television and 10 of them were in the Nielsen's top 20 programs. Clearly something important is revealed by these figures. It could be that we are seeking escapism in humor—but why in situation comedy rather than some other kind? It may also be that these programs reflect certain changes that are taking place in our view of things, that the old egoistic self-reliant devil-take-the-hindmost individualism that we believed in for so long is on the wane and that we are all coming to a new view of the relation that exists between an individual and society.

Despite all their ersatz individuality, the comic heroes and heroines in situation comedies are all interchangeable, for personality becomes secondary in this form of humor. Freud explained this phenomenon in his *Jokes and Their Relation to the Unconscious*:

The characteristics of the person who provides the comic effect do not in this case play an essential part; we laugh even if we have to confess that we should have had to do the same in that situation. We are here extracting the comic from the relation of human beings to the often over-powerful external world; and this external world also comprises social conventions and necessities and even his bodily needs.

Thus, we can, to use Freud's term, detach the comic from the character and by manipulation put him into situations in which his *actions* are subject to comic conditions.

In situation comedies the individual is of secondary importance; he is not so much an actor as one who is acted upon, and is generally a victim of circumstances. Sitcoms can have many formats—in some the males are weak nincompoops, in some there are no males (a formula that allows both domestic comedy and the comedy of romance). The men who are heroes of domestic sitcoms are symbolically castrated, usually by the women and children in the stories, both of whom know better than he does.

Ten years ago sitcoms were at the peak of their popularity, and there were several dozen on at the same time. They generally lost their popularity, but now seem to be coming on strong again. This may be because television is faddish and different kinds of television programs (the western, the detective story, and others) have cycles of popularity. It may also be because the audience's attention span is limited to half an hour. But I don't think either of these explanations adequately explains the significance of sitcoms. It is probably because these programs reinforce everyone's identity loss, though in reassuring ways.

The irony of situation comedy—and especially a pro-

gram like *Rhoda*—is that it represents the reversal of the myth of the American as "nature's nobleman," as a clean-cut, hard-working, rugged, self-reliant individual who achieves his goals through force of willpower and determination. What we find are a collection of weak-willed, middle-class castrati or neurotic losers who find themselves in awkward situations all the time.

The women vary greatly, but within predictable parameters. We find beautiful women who can't get married or plain ones who can't even make it to their own weddings on time. Television, we all know, burns up comedians with voracity. Few of them last very long. Yet American audiences demand comedy and light programs. The answer then is to create a formula in which there is no personality to burn up; only humorous situations which keep on occurring. This, in turn, suggests that we see personality as finite and circumstance as infinite—and perhaps as more interesting.

*Rhoda* is really a study in the banality of the counter-cliché. Its formula is opposition to the prevailing formulas, but it is no less artificial and unreal than the typical situation comedy it tries to repudiate. We might look at a typical formula for a situation comedy and contrast *Rhoda* with it.

| | CLASSICAL SITCOM | RHODA |
|---|---|---|
| TYPE OF INDIVIDUAL | No individuals. Situations basic. | Pseudo-individuals. |
| CHARACTERS | Weak males, dominant females posited as normal. | Neurotics, losers posited as normal. |
| RELATION TO SOCIETY | Overwhelmed by society and circumstances. Mom and kids know best. | Circumstance basic. |

|  | CLASSICAL SITCOM | RHODA |
|---|---|---|
| ACTION | Slapstick, unbelievable and overtly so. | Slapstick, unbeliev-able but covertly so. |
| LOVE | Male is "naughty child" or castrated. | Male strong on outside. |
| AMBIENCE | Sentimental. | Antisentimental. |

In *Rhoda* we find a classic error. She thinks she is being individualistic when she is really being cynical and antisocial. She makes lots of cutting remarks about everyone, though we all know that underneath that hard exterior beats the proverbial heart of gold. The same applies to Joe. There is one scene that reveals the fraud in *Rhoda*. Rhoda is describing Joe to Mary and telling how wonderful he is. Mary is ecstatic, saying she just knows Joe must be something wonderful. All of a sudden the door opens and Joe bursts in, cussing and angry and *seeming* to be a terrible brute! He is presented as a rather gross individual. However, this preliminary impression turns out to be misleading and he is next shown in a much more softened and gentle manner. Yes, underneath his gruff exterior, *too,* Joe is someone genuinely loving and warm.

The fundamental thing about *Rhoda* is that it is as sentimental and meretricious as any of the patently silly situation comedies. But it must be faulted because it takes itself more seriously, it claims to raise our consciousness, it asserts its basic truthfulness. Thus *Rhoda* must be judged more harshly than other situation comedies, which are only trying to get as many laughs as they can. The ultimate sentimentalism in *Rhoda* is that it is not serious about life. It is only when you recognize the tragic dimensions of life

that you can appreciate its comic aspects, and can create great comedy. *Rhoda* is ultimately as trivial as all of its counterparts, except that it mistakes the overt display of hostility and aggressivness as being truthful and serious.

Many people fail to distinguish between solemnity and seriousness. But just because a person is solemn (and presents himself to the world with solemnity and reserve), it does not follow that he is serious. And just because a person is lighthearted and gay, we must not assume he is not serious. The popular mind, however, cannot make the distinction between solemnity and seriousness, and thus is led to think it has had profound experiences when it has only had solemn (or sentimental) ones. In the same way, because Rhoda makes cutting remarks and is snide, people tend to assume they are getting reality—as if hostility were inextricably linked with truthfulness.

The hidden sentimentality in *Rhoda* stems from its fundamental assumption that life is comic and that everything must end happily. *Rhoda* is a great success and has been described as an instant hit. I would say this is so because it fosters our illusions and plays upon our absurd notions about the nature of reality. When anything and everything is turned into comedy, comedy becomes diluted and nothing is particularly funny. The program will probably remain popular for a number of years; but with each situation Rhoda and Joe will become less real. For if the format involves the matter of Rhoda and Joe (and Mary Tyler Moore, as well) extricating themselves from *circumstances,* which are basic and are posited as fundamental, the more shows we see the less real the characters become. The final triumph of situation comedy is that it depersonalizes the actors and the viewers, so that what we are

laughing at, really, is our own psychic destruction. We laugh at the realization that we don't count.

In America, however, this is ironic and not tragic since, as I've pointed out in my treatment of *Mission Impossible,* Americans do not have a tragic sense of life.

## ★ brown skin but white soul

*Chico and the Man* was one of the hits of the 1974 season. It was an immediate sensation and turned a relatively obscure actor, Freddie Prinze, into a star. As a review of the program in *Time* put it, in an article called "The Prinze of Prime Time":

> *My parents met on the subway—picking each other's pockets.*
>
> *My mother's always talking about the wedding. "You shoulda been there," she says. She doesn't remember. I was there, and so were my two brothers.*
>
> *To survive in the ghetto, you gotta look tough. The best way to look tough is to have a broken arm.*

Bill Cosby? Dick Gregory? Or maybe Richard Pryor

in one of his less savage moments? Wrong, wrong, wrong. It is ghetto humor all right, but it comes from a different part of town—the streets of the Latino section of Manhattan's Upper West Side, where a fat kid named Freddie Prinze lived for most of his twenty short years. Nowadays Freddie works another *barrio*. As the wisecracking Chicano hustler in the decrepit East Los Angeles garage in NBC's smash new series *Chico and the Man*, Prinze is the hottest new property on prime-time TV.

Prinze is a superb comic and his talent is one of the reasons for the success of the program. But *Chico and the Man* is popular for other reasons.

The program really deals with the redemption of a lost soul—Ed Brown, a self-destructive, cantankerous bigot who owns a run-down garage in the middle of a Los Angeles Chicano ghetto. He is a bitter man who cannot come to terms with himself or his daughter, and finds solace in humiliating his occasional customers and in drinking. That is, his free-floating hostility manifests itself in aggressive actions against others and himself. As a symbolic figure it might be argued that he represents the classic White Anglo Saxon Protestant (WASP) American, who finds, suddenly, that America is not what he thought it was. America is not all-white; instead there are all those black and brown men and women around him, and by a quirk of fate, Brown finds himself surrounded by them, as much a prisoner of the ghetto as they are.

There is a dialectic set up, then, between Ed Brown (the name is ironic), this symbol of arid Protestantism, and Chico, a Chicano hustler who sees a chance to make something of his life by entering into "partnership" with Brown. Brown has let his shop run down, he lacks will, he is ener-

vated. Into this morbid scene comes Chico, full of spirit, full of life. He surveys the ruin that Brown has made of his shop (and his life) and sets to work, immediately, to salvage things. And he won't take no for an answer.

Chico fascinates us because he offers a glimpse, even if highly romanticized, of what might be called "street life." He is a street person who must live by his wits, and a rather exotic type for the average American. We know now, from studies that have been made of street-corner societies and ghetto life, that inhabitants of the ghetto are incredible actors who have evolved a number of techniques for dealing with elements of society representing power and authority. To the ordinary middle-class American who has security (or seemed to have it until the economic depression of the mid-seventies) these people in the ghetto have something of the fabulous about them. They eat strange foods, have exotic women who frequently attract us (because we feel we can have sexual relations with them without guilt), and give our drab society a bit of character and perhaps color.

We feel ambivalent about our ethnic minorities; we are unsure about them. Because the media have for so long, focused upon white Americans we have become habituated to think of Americans as white. Now, thanks to the civil rights movement and the upsurge in ethnic pride in America, this is changing. Still, we don't know, for certain, what to make of all these Latinos and Chicanos who speak foreign languages and seem so utterly different from us. Some of our feelings about ethnic groups are more conditioned by class differences than anything else. That is, for example, the association we make between Chicanos, and other ethnic groups and dirt. Americans see themselves as

"clean" and others as "dirty." In the pilot script, for example, just after Ed has met Chico, the following conversation takes place: Chico tells Ed that his garage looks like a "basurero," which he explains is a junkyard. Ed tells him to go away and take his "flies" with him. When Chico asks him "which flies?" Ed tells him, "You people got flies all around you" and adds that Chico's flies and his flies are getting together and "making more flies."

There is also a connection between dirt and sexuality revealed here, which is most interesting. I'm not sure whether many of our antagonisms about ethnic groups (dirty Poles and dirty Jews and dirty Chicanos) are because of class differences or ethnic differences. Because many ethnic groups tend to be working class, it is hard to separate ethnicity from class, and to discern which of the two middle-class Americans find so distasteful. It may be the case that they find *both* ethnicity and working-class life styles disgusting.

The connection between ethnics being dirty and having a flamboyant sexual life is revealed in the dialogue quoted above. For many Americans there are all kinds of myths about the sexual life of people in the ghetto, and fantasies about Super-Niggers and Super-Mexicans. The problem is complicated by the matter of machismo, the belief found in certain subcultures that male potency is manifested by sexual conquest, large families, and other such factors. But it seems quite likely that part of the hostility found in the white middle-class community toward ethnics stems from a resentment and jealousy about their sexual practices. They "breed like flies," many Americans believe, and the middle-class Americans have to pay for it all.

Of course many of the ethnic elements in our society find Chico very comforting. He is, after all, an heroic individual, and the dominating presence in the show. Ed Brown owns the garage (just as the WASPs "own" the country), but his power is not real; he has the illusion of power, but it is Chico who really runs things. Ed Brown is old and tired and actually incapable of surviving on his own. He is not totally corrupt; in fact, underneath it all he has redeeming features. But he is a lost soul on his own —and without Chico to salvage and maintain him, Ed Brown would "self-destruct," to use the jargon of the space age.

Could it be that *Chico and the Man* is a parable about the redemption of a neurasthenic culture by the introduction of new blood, of yet another—or perhaps newly visible —wave of ethnics with exotic ways and tastes who will regenerate a thin and tired society? Could it be that the age of the WASP has passed? That the blue-collar workers, the ethnics, the unwelcome visitors will take over, just as Chico has taken over and, in his own subtle way, dominates "the Man"? The people in the Chicano ghetto use exotic spices and eat remarkable foods. The Mexican-Americans know about spices, they know what subtlety is, what heat is, and they thrive in a land of instant mashed potatoes, frozen peas, television dinners, and instant food. The primal, undifferentiated American appetite recognizes that it is missing something, that it has little scope, and into the void have leaped the ethnics and the exotics.

The curious thing about *Chico and the Man* is that we find the ethnics full of what used to be characteristics of the WASP: drive and initiative. It is Chico who has ambition and energy; Ed Brown, who we may take as a symbol

of American culture in general, is tired and bankrupt, in every sense of the word. He cannot come to terms with his daughter, with his neighbors, or with himself—and tries to annihilate himself by alcoholism. He is lost. And it is Chico who saves Ed Brown, who allows him to kindle once again the flame of humanity latent within him.

In a very real sense *Chico and the Man* represents a retelling of the Horatio Alger story. A poor but energetic little fellow shows he's got drive and imagination and is soon on his way to success. Like one of Alger's heroes, Chico saves somebody—in this case the leading figure (rather than his daughter or some other child) and outwits hostile forces. And like a typical Alger hero he has an honest face and disarming manner; in the Alger world, personality is one of the keys to success, and Chico, like Ragged Dick or any other Alger hero, has plenty of charisma. That's what it takes to survive in a hostile world . . . plus some "luck, pluck, and virtue."

In a sense, then, it can be said that *Chico and the Man* is a reaffirmation of the American Dream, of the possibility for people to rise in the world so long as they have the right combination of sufficient willpower and a bit of luck. Every racial and ethnic group has found itself down at the bottom of the totem pole and has had the opportunity to rise in the world. In the case of the Negroes, the Chicanos and Latinos, the Native Americans, and a few other groups, it has been hard going. But the belief that any individual *can* succeed, perhaps in spite of his race, is a dominant theme in American culture. This myth of the self-made man, the so-called American Dream, is just that—a myth, a dream—but it still holds a strong grip upon our imagination, and it has had great impact upon our society and our

institutions. Thus *Chico and the Man* is more than a funny series about a Chicano youth and a crusty old man. The title is very suggestive: an individual, Chico, and "the Man," which, in the ghetto, stands for white Americans in general.

The program is informed by a dialectic, which is shown below:

| Chico | the Man |
|---|---|
| youth | old age |
| ethnicity | white Anglo-Saxon Protestantism |
| life | death (self-destructiveness) |
| integration | alienation |

Of course neither Ed Brown nor Chico is a perfectly representative figure, but in terms of the program they both are symbolic manifestations of the average American and the typical ghetto dweller. The notion that young people will "save" older people is also a fundamental principle, so it seems, in contemporary American culture. Of course Chico has internalized our basic American values; he wants to get out of the ghetto. He is a "Super-Mex" who wants to be "associated with this floundering enterprise," as he puts it when he first confronts Ed Brown. He's a Vietnam War veteran with a Silver Star who wants a "place in the sun." By force of personality and persistence, Chico becomes a partner in the garage, and the bond between him and Ed is more than simply an economic one. They are people whose lives and destinies are mixed together; you cannot get rid of Chico by insulting him or being nasty. He won't go away, and neither will all his friends and relations in the *barrio*.

In his brilliant study of Mexican life and thought, *The*

*Labyrinth of Solitude,* Octavio Paz discusses *pachucos,* "youth, for the most part of Mexican origin, who form gangs in Southern cities; they can be identified by their language and behavior as well as by the clothing they affect." These *pachucos,* says Paz, face a dilemma: they do not wish to become Mexicans again and yet they don't won't to "blend into the life of North America," and lose what little identity they have. Chico, we can see, is not a *pachuco* in any sense of the term. He has brown skin but a white soul and a bourgeois point of view. In a sense, then, he represents a very conservative point of view. He has enough Mexican blood in him to escape from many of the destructive elements of the American Way of Life, but underneath it all he seems to be trying to selling his birthright for a bowl of pottage.

Chico can suceed in America, but to do so he must sacrifice a great deal. His Mexican-ness is as phony in the program as it is in Freddie Prinze, who is half-Hungarian and half-Puerto Rican—Prinze calls himself a Hungar-Rican. The dilemma Chico faces, to put it bluntly, is how to reconcile his Mexican spirit with his Puritan soul.

## ★ a case study in the world of children's television

One evening as I was putting my son Gabriel to bed, we happened to find ourselves discussing dreams. "What are dreams?" I asked. "Pictures in your sleep," he answered, being a typical eight-year-old. "And where are those pictures?" I said. He thought for a moment, and replied, "In your head!" Continuing the conversation I then asked, "What do you usually dream about?" He blushed and hesitated, and gave me an evasive answer. "Come on," I asked. "I really want to know. I'm curious." "Well," he said, snuggling in his bed, "I always dream about the same thing. I dream of Batman."

I only allow him to watch one hour of television a day, and he likes Batman, so that program represents half of

a normal day's viewing time. He is not always faithful to *Batman* but frequently watches it. It turns out he dreams he is an inventor who helps Batman by inventing various things for him to use. I decided to watch *Batman*—I'd not seen it for years—and this is what I saw.

I am listing everything I saw from the moment my son switched on the set (I took notes to see if I could capture a typical experience):

1. An advertisement for Mattel toys.

2. Previews of programs that were appearing.

3. *The introduction to Batman, featuring the cartoon figures (upon whom the series is built), the characters in the day's adventures, and the characters who play Batman and Robin).*

4. An advertisement for Carrier's U-Fly-It.

5. An advertisement for Ultra-Chrome Racers (yea, man, they're cool).

6. An advertisement for Trix cereal.

7. *A segment of the program, which lasted about ten minutes.*

8. An advertisement for Lego toys.

9. An advertisement for Freakies cereal.

10. An advertisement for Sock'em Bump'em.

11. An advertisement for Trix cereal.

12. An advertisement for Bonanza, which would be shown later.

13. *A segment of the program, which lasted about ten minutes.*

14. An advertisement for Batman and Robin toys.

15. An advertisement for McDonald's gift certificates.

16. An advertisement for Rock'em Sock'em Robots.

17. An advertisement for Planet of the Apes toys.

18. *A short segment of the program.*

It is estimated that children are exposed to as much as 25 percent more advertising per hour than adults, though the stations, with great reluctance, are cutting down on this. And the techniques employed in the ads, the way they assault children with fantastic claims and unrealistic promises, only make the situation that much worse. If you multiply a list such as this by two or four or eight, you can gain some kind of a sense of what children's television is like.

Since the average child watches three or four hours per day, you must multiply this list by eight, and you come up with something like 150 commercials *per day*; and this figure is conservative since I didn't count advertising *after* the Batman program.

Batman is a very interesting phenomenon. When it appeared on television originally, in 1966, it was a resounding success and attracted enormous audiences. It was broadcast as an adult's program and became something of a camp cause célèbre. It appeared on Wednesday and Thursday evenings and was championed as a classic put-on. There was an element of the death of the heroic in this treatment; adults find it very hard to take comic-strip figures seriously, so the program relied on overstatement and absurdity to mask its ego problems. How can an actor take such a role seriously? And how can adults follow a program about comic-strip figures without feeling, somehow, childish? The

solution was to destroy Batman's original comic-strip personality and create a humorous version of the hero.

However, in doing this the producers destroyed the program, for people cannot tolerate put-ons and self-ridicule for extended periods of time; Batman quickly became a bore. To children who do not recognize the fact that Batman was a spoof, it still retains its credibility—and that may explain why the program is now shown to children, and is not popular as a rerun for adults. As Adam West, the actor who played Batman described the program:

> We're doing it satirically, but in a very special sense. It's satirical as far as tendency toward style. And certainly satirical as far as exaggeration and overstatement are concerned. But the rudiment here is to play with the truth. You might say my job is to make the overstatement as subtle as possible . . . I like to think of myself as nature's nobleman, with a sole desire to stamp out crime.

This description is interesting, since it ties Batman to the American myth of the natural hero. The name Adam (first man) West is also symbolic. Batman is revealed to be an Adamic hero—important since Americans have traditionally defined themselves as new Adams, innocent souls seeking salvation in a world of corruption and degeneracy. This theme is central to the American novel and is dealt with in a book by R.W.B. Lewis appropriately called *The American Adam*. The book deals with nineteenth-century fiction, but it also applies to the contemporary American scene.

Batman is a mythic figure who relates directly to very deeply felt currents in our culture—he is a vengeance figure, a caped crusader who personifies the traditional belief we have (stemming from our pietistic background) that we must scourge evil from the land. But in the tele-

vision program this feeling of responsibility is distorted and turned on its face into comedy and absurdity. The stiffness and crudeness that are found in the earliest Batman comics are reflected in the awkwardness and silliness of the program, except that the comic book was serious.

In the television series crime is comic, and the grotesques who serve as the "master criminals" are little more than clowns. The program is pervaded by a sense of absurdity and foolishness, and is full of gags that children cannot fathom (buying horses in glue factories, and using obviously pretentious language such as "expletives will get you nowhere.") Is it a mark of our maturity that we have relegated Batman to the children? American taste may have changed and programs as silly as it was can no longer find an adult audience (though programs equally as silly and trivial do). But it makes me wonder what American taste was like ten years ago, when Batman was so popular.

What strikes me most, however, is the fact that a program as ridiculous and silly as Batman can have such a hold on my son and capture his imagination so strongly that he dreams of the program. I cannot help but wonder what effect all those slick commercials are having on him, even though he knows he cannot expect to be given the cereals and toys that are advertised. And what effect do other programs have, programs that are more realistic and perhaps even more effective in stimulating him? Batman is played in a tongue-in-cheek manner. We find melodrama, comic names (Lola Lasagna), grotesque figures (the Penguin), bombastic and inflated language, comic alliteration, silly situations—and yet my son dreams of Batman.

One reason that Batman may appeal to children is that he represents a traditional comic figure, the depreciated

father, and as such, appeals to unconscious needs that are very strong but also deeply buried within them. In *Beyond Laughter,* Martin Grotjahn offers the following explanation of the relationship between comedy and the subconscious:

> The thesis is simple, straightforward, and convincing: the tragic guilt of the son is displaced upon the father. In comedy it is the father who is guilty. This inversion of guilt can be seen in Shakespeare's classic comedies as in all others. The villain is the victim of his own villainy; the cheat is cheated. The son is not rebellious but victorious. The son is not impotent, but the father is impotent, castrated, conquered. The son does not compete; but the weak and ridiculous father tries to do all the things which the son tried to do in the original tragic setting of the drama. The son plays the role of the father, and the father is cast in the role of the son. The result is amused superiority, laughing aggression, triumph without remorse, guilt or fear of punishment.

Batman is not only Robin's "father," but he is everyone's spiritual father, and everyone (who watches the program, that is) is his spiritual son. He is a mixture of the heroic and the comic, a figure to emulate and imitate but also to transcend. (The stage name of the actor who plays Robin, Burt Ward, is appropriate here and must have been taken with Robin's role in mind.) Batman is the ridiculous father who doesn't recognize that he is absurd now, that he must be replaced, and it is all the young children of America, who go running around shouting "Batman! Batman!" who are prepared to step into his shoes and do a really good job of capturing criminals and fighting crime.

In the analysis I made of Batman in my book, *The*

*Comic-Stripped American,* (New York: Walker and Company, 1973) I suggested that he was what I called "a spiritual orphan." He is one of a legion of orphans who populate the comics and who spend their lives warring on crime. Now I have suggested he is also a spiritual father and I believe that is the case, though I am not speaking literally. This theme, that of the spiritual orphan, is one which I believe informs American culture and deserves our attention. The spiritual orphan is connected with the theme of abandonment. In my discussion of *The Yellow Kid,* our first comic strip, I said:

> The kids in *The Yellow Kid* are abandoned—left to their own devices by parents presumably too busy, or too tired, to look after them. This theme, that of the "abandoned" child, is a recurrent one in the comics. We find many heroes and heroines in the comics who are abandoned for one reason or another. . . . This sense of having *been* abandoned is intimately related, I believe, to the American historical experience of *abandoning* the old world, our "fatherland," and coming to a new world where there were opportunities for improvement. There is a heavy psychological price to be paid for casting out on one's own—and the idea that one can and should do this is with us today; it may be that many runaways, hippies and sleeping-bag wanderers are dropping out on their own before they will be (so they feel) abandoned by their parents. . . .

Is this not the fate of our children, who are abandoned by their parents, left to wander through the vast and terrifying "wasteland" of television-land on their own? We are not dealing with characters in comic strips here, however, but with our own children. They are left to their own devices—the devices in this case being television sets.

We do this, in part, because our heads are full of

myths about our kids and the way they respond to television. Most people grasp at these myths (which I am defining here as "erratic notions") because they justify neglect by parents, and relieve them of guilt feelings.

MYTH ONE: KIDS KNOW BEST. It may be true that children, as well as adults, can discern "fakes" on television —though I don't believe it is true. How many people selling cereal or soap powder believe what they say? And these wonderfully perceptive kids don't even perceive that Batman is pulling their legs. But even if it were true that you can't fool kids, it doesn't mean that they can discriminate between good and bad programs. They will watch junk when they can, and eat junk when they can—and it probably is the case that a great deal of the junk they eat is connected to the junk they see! Although we are a very wealthy country, the diet of large numbers of people is seriously deficient. As someone who knows something about the subject said to me recently, "If we don't want half the country to starve to death, we may have to fortify Coca-Cola and Twinkies."

Kids don't know what's best for them. If they did, they wouldn't watch television the way they do.

MYTH TWO: TELEVISION NETWORKS CARE. Television networks are profit-making entities and have not shown very much responsibility as far as the programs they have created for children are concerned. The same applies to local, independent television stations. At best these networks are careless (if you want to give them the benefit of the doubt), and at worst they are exploitative and cruel. They inflict many more minutes of commercials upon children (per hour) than they would dare to inflict upon adults, and have not demonstrated a sense of responsibility

for the products they advertise. For a while they showed commercials for children's vitamin pills and only took such commercials off the air when the public outcry over the creation of pill-popping in children grew too loud.

When you compare the quantity and quality of children's television programming in America with that in Great Britain, for example, you cannot avoid coming to the conclusion that the situation here is simply scandalous. The British show great sensitivity to the needs of children and tailor their television programs to these needs; the children are not bombarded with commercials the way they are here.

The television networks and stations defend themselves against the charge that they are exploiting young people with their advertisements and harming them by exposing them to programs saturated with violence by making one claim: television only gives people "what they want," and television is only a reflection of the outside world. This view can be challenged. As Scott Ward of Harvard's Marketing Science Institute pointed out in "Effects of Television Advertising on Adolescents: Preliminary Research Results":

> I must seriously question a theory of mass communications effects which says, essentially, that the mass media merely reinforce existing attitudes and predispositions of audience members. It all depends on what kinds of effects you are looking for. If your measure of mass media effects is attitude change—that ubiquitous variable in social psychological experiments—then you will probably conclude that television doesn't affect youngsters and teenagers much. But why should it? Youngsters and teenagers are presumably in the process of *attitude formation*. As such, they do not have firm attitudes, and to look for changes in atti-

tudes would lead you to the erroneous conclusion that the media have no effects.

Clearly the media do have effects on children and teenagers, but these effects have to do with *learning* and formation of ideas about the world.

Since we abandon our children to the television wasteland and leave them to fend for themselves, is it any wonder they become, in a real sense, strangers? If the average child watches fifty hours of television per week (or about 64 percent of his waking time) is it any wonder that Batman is his father?

MYTH THREE: THE GOVERNMENT WILL PROTECT US. Would that it were so! Unfortunately the Federal Communications Commission, like most governmental commissions, is a captive of the industry. It was created to protect the public interest—since, in fact, the public owns the airwaves. All radio stations and television stations are making use of public property, and should be regulated in the interest of the American people. Instead the commission has become the servant of the industry, like most Federal commissions.

In part this is because such commissions tend to be made up of experts from the industry being regulated, who are naturally sympathetic to the wants and needs of the industry and are predisposed toward it. In addition, in the case of the Federal Communications Commission for instance, the members may not be sensitive to the psychological and social significance of the media, and in all cases give media the benefit of the doubt. The burden of proof is shifted from the television networks, which are using public airwaves, to critics and groups of people who find fault with various aspects of television: the programs, the advertise-

ments, hiring of minority groups, and other factors. Some progress is being made, thanks to the formation of organizations such as Action for Children's Television, but the stations are wealthy and powerful, and the system is structured so that change is very hard to effect. Let me quote from a *New York Times* article in this regard:

> In one of his final opinions as an appeals court judge, Warren E. Burger, the new chief justice, delivered a harsh rebuke to the Federal Communications Commission and withdrew the broadcasting license of a Mississippi television station that had been accused of racially discriminatory programming. . . .
>
> In overturning that renewal, Burger's opinion restated his concern that the FCC has a built-in prejudice in favor of established broadcasters and has forgotten its responsibility to the public interest.
>
> The opinion said that the FCC's examiner had revealed "a curious neutrality-in-favor-of-the-licensee" (WLBT) in his conduct of the evidentiary hearings on the case. The opinion further charged the FCC members with distorting the burden of proof to protect the station from its challengers.

Thus, we can see that the government won't protect us and neither will Batman. In fact, the government won't even protect us *from* Batman.

The networks make another argument, relevant to this matter, which I would like to discuss. "Parents," the network tell us, "you are in control of your household. You can determine what your children will watch. After all, you can always switch channels or turn the set off."

MYTH FOUR: PARENTS CAN CONTROL TELEVISION WATCHING. This myth is based on two questionable matters: first, that parents "know best" what is good for their

children and second, that parents can "control" what their children watch. I question whether parents really do know what is good and bad as far as television programs are concerned; I doubt that they always do. But it doesn't matter since parents do not and cannot control what their children watch.

In principle, of course, the parents control the television set, but in fact, generally speaking, that is not the case. Children are allowed to choose what they want, most of the time, and their choice is geared to junk, most of the time. Let me quote from *Children's Television Fact Sheet* (April 25, 1971):

> The industry treats children as consumers. According to an article from *Broadcasting Magazine*, entitled "Partners for Profit: Children, Toys, and TV":
>
> "The objective of children's programming is to attract the largest possible audience at the lowest possible cost."
>
> The effect of the "rating war" approach means an emphasis on entertainment of a fast, crude, undemanding and highly stimulating sort that can hold the attention of all ages.

Since parents have very little control over their children, in general, why should they be able to control their television viewing? The genius of television, as a one-eyed baby sitter, is that it frees parents from having to be involved with their children, it gets kids out of their parents' hair. But what we do when we give our children free rein over the television set is to abandon them to the disruptive forces of their anarchistic impulses. Children need boundaries and limits, otherwise they feel lost.

Parents frequently lean over backward in allowing

their children freedom, and fear that they will smother their children by asserting parental authority. What happens, however, is that children interpret this so-called freedom as abandonment, and are miserable. They lack centrality and ego development and are pulled in conflicting directions by their anarchistic impulses. The ironic result, then, is that permissive parents, who relinquish their authority, end up with children who are disturbed, who feel unwanted and unloved. For these children Batman may be more "real," as a parental authority figure, than their actual fathers.

One of the areas in which parents abdicate their responsibility is in television viewing. As long as the kids are quiet, and not a bother, the parents are happy. But, I would suggest, these parents do not know what price they are paying, because they are unable to recognize how their children feel and are unaware of the power of television. This leads us to the next myth.

MYTH FIVE: TELEVISION DOESN'T MAKE THAT MUCH DIFFERENCE. When all else fails, we can fall back on this argument. Television is, after all, only one socializing factor. There are others, such as the home and family, school, peer groups, and religion. But the child doesn't spend the amount of time with peer groups, in churches and religious establishments, or even with his family that he does with television. A great deal of his time at home is spent watching television. So much of his socialization by the family is taken over by television, and Batman, his spiritual father, may be more important to him than his real father.

I have already commented upon the fact that Batman is a depreciated figure, and we all recognize that male figures in many programs have become softened and

weakened—when not eliminated, that is. The consequences of this are considerable. For as Milton Sapirstein points out in "The Neurotic Child from the Happy Home" from *Paradoxes of Everyday Life*:

> If we compare the democratic home with its authoritarian predecessor, the most striking feature appears to be the decline in the father's prestige. He who was once the Jehovah of the family cosmos—remote, awe-inspiring, at once law-giver and judge—has dwindled into a minor Deity. Mother and children no longer tremble before him; as a matter of fact, he would be embarrassed if they did. He is a familiar figure around the house, now, a good guy who helps out with the dishes and diapers, plays games with the children and rarely stands on his dignity. . . .
>
> The deflation of the father [however] may lead to serious maladjustments in the development of his children. His sons, particularly, may suffer. To become men in their turn, they must have an effective masculine figure with which to identify. Only so can they resolve successfully the crucial conflict of the oedipal period when they must break away finally from the infantile needs and desires which cluster around the mother. If the father's image is weak or blurred, if he lacks authority, it is much harder for them to make the great renunciation.
>
> Fear of his contempt or anger plays a vital part in establishing the necessary inner controls. Pride in his strength and identification with it—"I, too, am a man"—compensates the boy for the sacrifice of his childish fantasies and encourages him to embark upon his masculine identity.

It is to these needs that Batman, our spiritual father, speaks. And what is he—a clown who cannot take himself seriously, who injects absurd melodrama into trivial situations, who ultimately forces us to recognize him for what

he is—a fool. And what do the legions of children who love Batman feel when the great recognition comes? What must they think? Perhaps something like this:

> Batman, my father, I really loved you. I loved the way you captured the Penguin and all those other bad guys, and I loved the fights you and Robin got into, and I loved the Batmobile and the Bat Cave, and all those incredible machines and things you had. And boy, was I scared and angry about the way the Penguin glued you and Robin in the Batmobile, and the dirty tricks the Joker and the other meanies tried to play on you.
>
> I always recognized that there was something different from the way you were in your comic book, because there the Joker was a real fiend and murdered people left and right, and the way you were on television. I loved the action, even though I didn't like the idea of having a Batgirl spoiling the fun.
>
> And then one day, Batman, my father, I suddenly realized that you really didn't mean anything, that you were just making believe, and making fun of me. You weren't really strong and dynamic at all. In fact, you were weak and dumb. Batman, my father, you were just like my real father.

## ★ or the secret of the wheelchair

Living with the reality that two-thirds of the crimes known to police and over half the murders committed in America are never solved, we enjoy . . . detective stories, where evil characters are always stopped. The fantasy satisfactions of the stories may help us feel more secure about the unlikelihood of someone taking away what we have. Like a neurotic with a repetition compulsion, we watch the good triumph over the bad, over and over again.

—CHARLES WINICK,
*The New People*

According to the *Random House Dictionary of the English Language, ironside* refers to "a person with great power

of endurance or resistance." They also say that the name or nickname *Ironsides* was given to Oliver Cromwell. But our Ironside is a strange person, an invalid confined to a wheelchair—who happens to be a detective with the police in San Francisco, that Sodom by the bay. His name is strange and seems to have a number of levels of meaning.

There is an element of irony in his situation; he is a man of action who is confined to a wheelchair. Confined is the basic metaphor. He captures criminals who then are confined to rooms with iron sides. The series is based on a procedural detective format; closure is the essence of the stories, as Chief Ironside and his team track down evildoers who are then put behind iron bars. The criminals start with complete liberty; they have all the space they need, but as the drama progresses they find themselves hunted until, finally, they are caught and have no space for maneuvering. There is no escape and retribution is inevitable.

His wheelchair is what gives Ironside a distinct identity. He is instantaneously recognizable and easily parodied by comedians, thanks to this device. The problem of identity is critical in detective dramas, for if a program is to be successful, the hero must stand out in some way, must be distinctive. Otherwise he will be lost in the clutter of other heroes, an anonymous figure with no claim to fame. Thus, in recent years, the White Anglo-Saxon Protestant detective, with classic features and model personality, has given way to Italians in sloppy raincoats, bald Poles who suck lollypops, and other such types.

The iron wheels of his wheelchair are iron sides that Chief Ironside must contend with. But though these wheels may limit his lateral motion, he can move forward with relative ease. Motion yet repose, that is his secret. He is not

involved in "leg work"—he has his team of a black, a white, and a woman to do this—but "mind work," for that is what chief investigators do. He is the Cromwell, the strategist, and the team is his troops, his "roundheads" waging war for the glory of God.

As a "brilliant cripple" he represents a common notion in the popular imagination, that there is balance in nature and people who lose one faculty frequently make it up by developing other faculties. Thus it is perfectly reasonable to find the combination of an atrophied body and a brilliant mind. The sniper's bullet that paralyzed Ironside from the waist down freed him to think more clearly and, ironically, turned him into a more effective detective.

The American public believes this because it sees thought as divorced from action. It is a very romantic notion, reinforced, no doubt, by the mass media, which present thinkers as strange figures who can only function when they can remove themselves from the distractions of everyday life. Thought is somehow pure and ideas are magically plucked out of the ether. Ironside actually contradicts this notion, while, at the same time, reinforcing it.

*As a heroic figure Ironside, the brilliant cripple, represents rationality divorced from actuality*; yet in the program, he functions in just the opposite way. His decisions and orders are based on information he is given. That, after all, is the genius of the procedural detective story. Information, clues, bits and pieces of evidence are assembled and they lead to more information until the crime is solved. The detective in the *procedural* mystery (as against the *action* mystery, in which there is a great deal of violence, and chance and coincidence are critical) is a personification of science; he gets information, he constructs a theory, he

tests it out, and his success is a triumph of method and mind over chance.

Chief Ironside is not presented as the incarnation of rationality, as a "brain." Indeed, he is a warm and somewhat paternalistic figure, with strong human loyalties and feelings. But in this crippled detective we all recognize brillance. Had he been shot and crippled without any recompense it would have been a cruel and malicious event, it would not be congruent with our fundamental belief in the justness and morality of the universe. Ironside may have his body shot out from under him, but his iron will is resolute and his war on crime is both personal (justice) and cosmic (redemption of society); he is, we know, an instrument of divine judgment. He is "hell on wheels" to the criminal elements of the San Francisco area and other places he visits.

The dilemma of the procedural detective story is that to the extent it glorifies mind and rationality, it has to minimize action and violence; which means there is an inherent flatness to such stories, unless they are extremely well written. In one adventure, "Inside Job," a series of improbable errors are made by the criminals, who are masterminded, it turns out, by an inspector from Scotland Yard. He has his team of criminals rob three different places, but they only take $3,000 at each job. They then buy electric equipment, in San Francisco, which will enable them to bypass electric alarms constructed before a certain date. The police guard a number of banks and such, but the criminals steal Bolivian banknotes from a printing shop.

The salesman in the electronics store recognizes who bought the equipment, the criminals are inevitably apprehended (but not before one has killed another, to keep him

from talking) and the inspector dies from a heart attack. He discovered he was terminally ill but had three years to go before he got his pension . . . hence he tried to pull one job and get a nest egg by recovering the loot and framing someone he disliked, for some reason. Aside from the idea being a bit farfetched, the inspector would hardly have made the simple errors he did. (We know he is brilliant because he defeats Ironside, an old friend, in chess.)

During this episode, various clues are discovered and they help Ironside unravel the mystery. As we watch the program we know that the inspector from Scotland Yard is involved with the criminals, so the resolution of the episode is not startling. The story holds no great mystery and procedes in a rather banal way. Suspects are picked up, they confess, and that is that. Except for a bit of gratuitous violence, very little happens aside from a good deal of chasing around by Ironside and his assistants. The mystery in this episode involves *how* Ironside will track the criminals down. Procedural detective stories are not *"who done its"* in which a number of people have reasons for being suspected. The concern in procedural stories is with technique and with closure.

The difference between the master detective and ourselves is that he recognizes clues when he sees them. We may all see the same things, but because he has knowledge and experience, he is able to notice items that we pass over. We are confused because there is so much to consider that real clues become lost in the mass of things. A detective such as Ironside has more than mind to go on; he has laboratories, which can get him information, and he has sources who can interpret things for him. He does not rely *only* upon "the little grey cells" of Hercule Poirot, for

instance, but upon ballistic reports and witnesses to crimes. Rather than thinking things out, Ironside puts things together. He has too many guns in his armory, so to speak, for any criminal.

Why people should be so fascinated by mysteries is rather interesting, and there are a number of theories that have been put forth to explain the popularity of this form of popular culture in all the media. (It is estimated that about 25 percent of all books published are mysteries and there are a large number of detective mysteries on television.)

Some have suggested that such mysteries are reassuring. Inevitably the criminals are captured and the forces of law and order prevail; this reinforces our commitment to and belief in the justness of the universe, for though the forces of evil may seem to be triumphing, inevitably they will be defeated. Crime, we learn, over and over and over again, does not pay.

In addition to this ethical explanation, there is a psychoanalytic one, which argues that our interest in crime and mystery stories is connected with our interest in what went on in the parental bedroom. As Martin Grotjahn wrote in *Beyond Laughter*:

> The attempt to learn the facts of life is later symbolized in the search for the detailed facts of a crime, which lead to the discovery of the murderer. The interest in the mystery is a reactivation of the long-repressed interest in the bloody details of life and death, intercourse, menstruation, defloration, pregnancy, birth, delivery, and all the rest of it. The secret crime is the crime of the primal scene, which a child is not supposed to witness.

In mysteries our curiosity is "displaced from sex to crime,"

but we never fully gratify ourselves and solve the mystery, which leads to addiction.

Grotjahn explains the power of the detective as follows:

> The criminal investigation of the mystery story desexualizes our curiosity and idealizes it in the interest of justice. It is personified in the great detective who can investigate, combine, speculate, indulge in the infantile lust for uninhibited looking and listening without fear of reproach.

Although Grotjahn isn't talking about the kind of detective we find in Ironside, what he says applies to him. The gratifications we derive from Ironside may even be better, since he is an official investigator and functions with the sanction of society. He allows us to go along with him as he snoops; he is really a father figure who seems happy to teach us "the facts of life," though the aspects of life he teaches us about have little to do with the bedroom.

Young, tough-guy detectives, from the Freudian perspective, probably represent sons who want to crash their way into the bedroom. Ironside, a father figure, cannot get back into the bedroom, for he has been wounded—almost like a Hemingway hero—and is paralyzed from the waist down. He is impotent, and as such, no longer represents a threat to his rebellious sons and daughters. In terms of the Oedipal problem, he is the ideal father—the castrated one, who is confined to a wheelchair and only gets around thanks to the cooperation of his sons. He is a moral force to be reckoned with, however, and though we need not fear him as a physically punishing presence, he still is able to dominate us.

Detective programs (of which there are many on tele-

vision) allow us to resolve, to a certain degree, our conflicts about aggression. I have already suggested that these programs reinforce our superegos by demonstrating, over and over again, that criminals will inevitably be punished. But they also allow us to enjoy guilt-free aggression—both against society and against the criminal. We take part, vicariously, in the thrill of committing crimes, as we identify with the criminal; and we also enjoy and gain pleasure from his capture, when we identify with the detective.

In this case of Ironside our pleasure is rather diluted and watered down, since he is not a"hard" cop, not a tough guy, and he is also a wounded, weakened figure. He is not motivated by vengeance (though there is a ritualized reenactment of him being shot by a sniper at the beginning of each program) but has transcended such feelings; he represents a kind of philosophic understanding of man's frailty. As such, he cannot generate the kind of vicarious pleasures viewers get when they see tough detectives fighting hardened and violent criminals.

Ironside represents something foreign to the American experience in this regard. He recognizes human weakness and the existence of evil, and approaches it from a philosophic point of view. Most other detectives in American television approach crime differently. They are much more Protestant and see crime as a scourge to be attacked and eradicated, and do so with an evangelical frenzy. Thus, there is a great deal of emotional energy invested in finding the criminal and bringing him to justice; and doing so generates a great deal of satisfaction to the psyche.

In Ironside, however, I generally get the feeling that there is a certain reluctance involved in manhunting—in discovering who the criminal is, or in catching him (in epi-

sodes in which he is known to the viewers). Chief Ironside does not seem to take delight in his job; he pursues it with a kind of reticence, and a sense of sorrow. There is an element of softness about him, reflected partly in Raymond Burr's physical presence——he is slightly obese, almost fat. Chief Ironside is not morally soft in any way; he pursues criminals and captures them. It is, rather, that he does not take delight in the pursuit since he recognizes that we are all, in various ways, guilty; we are all sinners. He is, then, an anomaly in American culture, a philosophical and perhaps somewhat stoic figure in a world of driven, almost fanatic, perhaps even somewhat obsessed crime hunters. Our detectives represent personifications of our collective sense of guilt and they ravage our criminals as we ravage ourselves. Incapable of dealing with our aggressive and hostile emotions, we create fantasies in which we can work out our problems, but because we never really do come to grips with them, we are forever at the mercy of our creations. We hate them so that we need not hate ourselves, and because we cannot love ourselves, or even accept ourselves, we cannot do without them.

## ★ a romance of inner space

*Star Trek* is a classic space opera, the most interesting science fiction program television has created, and one which, remarkably enough, has refused to die. Though it is no longer being produced, its reruns are very popular and a vast audience of "Trekkers" exist, who relish these programs and put pressure on stations to carry them. The Trekkers even have a fan organization and publish a journal for aficionados of the program. It has taken on the characteristics of a cult.

The program deals with the adventures of the crew of the starship *Enterprise* on a five-year mission in outer space to explore new worlds, to seek out new civilizations, to "boldly go where no man has gone before." The word

*enterprise* has a number of meanings. According to the *Webster's Seventh New Collegiate Dictionary* it involves: 1) a project or undertaking that is difficult, complicated, or risky; 2a) a business organization; 2b) systematic, purposeful activity; 3) readiness to engage in daring action. The program actually comprehends all of these meanings, though the emphasis is upon adventure and risk.

Although the *Enterprise* is a starship (spaceship) and part of a vast fleet of such vehicles, it also is a self-contained little world; all ships are. It is commanded by Captain Kirk, a man of action and courage. He has two colleagues who are dominant in the series: Mr. Spock, the half-human, half-Vulcan science officer who represents "pure rationality," and "Bones" McKoy, the ship's physician, who represents feeling. The three form a triumvirate containing all the necessary ingredients for a heroic personality, except that they are distributed in three persons. Each of these figures is deficient in an important way, though as a team they are a formidable combination. The powers and deficiencies of these characters are charted below:

CHART I:
POWERS AND DEFICIENCIES OF CHARACTERS

| CHARACTER | POWERS | DEFICIENCY |
|---|---|---|
| Captain Kirk | action | reason, feeling |
| Mr. Spock | reason | action, feeling |
| Dr. McKoy | feeling | action, reason |

Ultimately, Kirk has to make decisions and take action, based upon knowledge and information from Spock and impressions from Dr. McKoy.

And what is remarkable is that despite the panoply of

technology and all the gadgets and gismos on the *Enterprise*, it is human courage that is ultimately decisive. The difference between Kirk and the various robots, presences, monsters, forces, whatever you will, that attack the starship and crew, is that humans have willpower and courage. When this is allied with superior information (from Mr. Spock) it must always triumph.

*Star Trek*, then, is not about science but rather human courage and boldness, working within certain parameters set by science and technology. Machines and technology form the backdrop, against which stories involving emotion, risk, madness, destructiveness, and courage are played out. Technology is a facilitating factor, but it does not really dominate men. It can't, otherwise aliens with superior technology would triumph, and that would be that. The division or dissociation of the psyche into three mutually exclusive (generally speaking) components is rather interesting, and suggests that each of our heroes is a manifestation of one component or part of what Freud calls our "psychical apparatus."

The following definitions (of the *id*, the *ego* and the *superego*) are taken from *The Random House Dictionary of the English Language* (The Unabridged Edition). First the *id*:

> The part of the psyche, residing in the unconscious, that is the source of instinctive energy. Its impulses, which seek satisfaction in accordance with the pleasure principle, are modified by the ego and the superego before they are given overt expression.

The second component of the psyche, the *ego*, is a portion of the *id* that undergoes special development, according to Freud. The *ego* is defined as:

The part of the psychic apparatus that experiences and reacts to the outside world and thus mediates between the primitive drives of the id and the demands of the social and physical environment.

Freud said, in *An Outline of Psycho-Analysis,* that the ego has control of voluntary movement and the ego's task is self-preservation. It stores up experiences in the memory, it avoids excessively strong stimuli by flight, it deals with moderately strong stimuli by adaptation, and it brings about changes in the world by activity.

The *superego* is defined as follows:

The part of the psychic apparatus which mediates between ego drives and social ideals, acting as a conscience which may be partly conscious and partly unconscious.

Freud believed that this was formed during childhood and that the superego represents "a special agency in which . . . parental influence is prolonged."

The superego has traditionally been identified with conscience, but it is much more than that since the superego functions on both a conscious and an unconscious level and passes judgment not only upon actions we intend to take, but also upon actions we do not recognize we intend to undertake. For our purposes we must stretch the concept of the superego slightly and suggest that it represents not only a moral judgment of what is acceptable, but also an intellectual assessment of what reality is like. We must split off the last part of the ego, as Freud described it above, and give this function to the superego—namely, acting in the world for the sake of survival.

If we do this, then we find that we can—without too much distortion—connect Kirk, Spock, and McKoy with

the three components of the psyche, the superego, the ego, and the id:

## CHART II:
## COMPONENTS OF THE PSYCHE AND CHARACTERS

| COMPONENT | MEANING | REALIZATION | CHARACTER |
|-----------|---------|-------------|-----------|
| super-ego | conscience | action | Capt. Kirk |
| ego | reason | intelligence | Mr. Spock |
| id | instinct | feeling | Dr. McKoy |

All charts represent oversimplifications and perhaps a bit of stretching, but I believe this chart does portray, graphically, the relation that exists between each character and the three components of the psyche, as Freud described them.

The fact that none of these characters is a "whole" man is important; we do not have a complete hero, a rounded man. Instead, we find aspects of the complete hero *dissociated* into three persons, each of whom represents one quality and is deficient in others. It may very well be that part of the popularity of the program stems from its delineation of characters who are radically flawed, who are not integrated, who are deficient in some important aspect, and in whom we recognize ourselves.

We are given good reason to understand why Mr. Spock is the way he is; he is half-Vulcan and therefore can be excused for lacking affect—or can he? He is, after all, half-human and as such should have some element of feeling. As a symbolic hero, he is most significant. He represents the emotional cripple, the mechanical man, the man who has such control of himself and his feelings that he seems to be a robot. As such he represents millions of people who find themselves in the same situation; *we are*

*afraid to have emotions, we suppress our feelings because we fear that if we do have feelings we must, inevitably, act on them, and these actions could be destructive.* In essence, we are afraid of going out of control and hurting people, since we identify feelings with aggression a great deal of the time. Consequently, we suppress our feelings, or our capacity to have feelings, and become robots. We also can get hurt if we have feelings, so we avoid rejection and hurt from others, though we are grievously doing damage to ourselves by bottling up our emotions.

Americans have many historical influences that have produced this character trait, or at least helped induce it. Our Puritan heritage certainly is important here, with its stress on self-restraint and the internalization of prohibitions. There is a great deal of discipline in the Puritan mind, and a narrowness, which has been distorted somewhat in evangelical movements that canalize emotion in very narrow channels. The feelings and emotions found in religious frenzy do not apply to interpersonal relations, generally speaking.

Spock, pure rationality, would find his counterpart in the Puritan saint, pure sanctity—and both would be freaks, monsters, whose ties with humanity would be most negligible. Neither Spock nor the Puritans attain the purity and narrowness they are identified with, however; Spock has human blood in his veins and the Puritans never were quite able to transcend their human limitations, though perhaps they would have liked to have done so. It is not much of a leap from the Puritans to the self-made man, who also has one goal—success—and who pursues this with such passion that there is little to his life but the pursuit. The self-made man represents a secularization of the Puri-

tan ethic, but the psychological dynamics are similar. The Puritan, the success-seeking zealot, and Spock are all the same—one-dimensional men, men without qualities but with one quality alone, that dominates them and gives them their identity.

There is but one area where the person who is not in touch with his feelings (this "person" may be the typical American, as a matter of fact) does allow himself the luxury of having emotions—romantic love, and, ironically, it may even be that our experience of romantic love is what convinces us to strangulate our feelings everywhere else. In contemporary American society we believe that romantic love is irresistible and all powerful, that it takes us where it will and we cannot control it. This belief, which sociologists have demonstrated to be sheer mythology, has two effects, both harmful. First, we concentrate too much of our emotional life on romantic love, which cannot stand up to the burdens placed upon it. We expect too much from it, because we have no place else where we feel free. Secondly, our belief that it is overpowering leads us to fear our emotions, to fear that they will get out of hand and will become devastating. (Unrequited love is painful, and emotions, in general, are dangerous.) Thus we become monsters of self-control and retreat into ourselves. Some, who are hurt in romantic love, become doubly convinced of the danger of emotions; they fear being hurt again and they fear hurting others.

What I have been describing represents a rather extreme situation, but I do believe that large numbers of Americans have problems with their emotions and fears of aggression and hurt. It is probably exacerbated here in America, where the Puritan influence is still so strong and

where Americans suffer from a general lack of sensory stimulation. The combination of sensory deprivation and unifocal psychic development poses enormous problems. We have little sense of our bodies, we have meager sensory stimulation (touch, smell, texture), and we avoid our feelings. *In extremo,* we are all Mr. Spocks, intelligence without emotion—except that not being Vulcanian we feel bad, somehow.

I have focused my attention upon Mr. Spock because he is the most interesting of the characters as far as his being "defined" is concerned. The Captain and Dr. McKoy are less focused and a bit more rounded, though they each symbolize a component of the psyche, as I have suggested. Mr. Spock, the human-Vulcanian, is a classic or textbook case, and his dilemma has similarities to that of the typical American who is afraid to get in touch with his emotions but unhappy because he finds his life unpleasant and drab.

At this point I would like to turn away from the psychological constellation in the characters (to a degree we have been dealing with inner space in outer space) to the subjects or themes found in the programs. I make a distinction between the plot of an episode and the theme or topic dealt with—which might be guilt or identity or retribution, for examples.

I will deal with a typical episode, "The Alternative Factor," as an example of the significance of themes in *Star Trek*. Generally speaking, interesting and important themes are raised in the program—in this case the theme is "duality." The story starts with the *Enterprise* being subjected to forces that Mr. Spock cannot explain. It turns out that the entire universe has also been subjected to some kind of "cosmic winking," and Captain Kirk is ordered to

investigate. A human presence is detected on an abandoned planet near the starship and when members of the crew beam down, they discover a small spaceship and a wild man, Lazarus, who screams "you've come . . . there's a chance to stop him. . . ." With that he faints and topples from a cliff. He is taken to the *Enterprise* and given medical attention. When he wakes he explains that he is devoting his life to chasing an evil *humanoid,* who lives only to destroy, who represents death, antilife, and must be stopped, for he has the capacity to annihilate universes at one stroke.

It turns out there are two Lazaruses—a good one who struggles with his alternative and evil other nature. The evil Lazarus is after power crystals in the *Enterprise,* which will enable him to destroy the universe, and the good Lazarus is constantly fighting to prevent this. The battle between Lazarus and his other nature are shown by negative instead of positive prints . . . and Lazarus nates between evil and goodness, as one or the ot. ments within him takes command.

The explanation of how the two Lazaruses ex how the evil one can annihilate the universe is rather plicated. It turns out that there is an alternative univ. or, to be more precise, a parallel universe to our one. Ours is matter and the other universe is antimatter. If Lazarus can bring the antimatter universe into contact with the regular universe, matter and antimatter will cancel themselves out. The cosmic winking involved a rip in the universe and represented a corridor, so to speak, between the alternative universes. Ultimately, with the aid of Captain Kirk, the evil Lazarus is forced into the corridor where he will spend eternity locked in struggle with the good Lazarus, and both universes will be preserved.

Obviously this is a rather complex story, both in terms of the physics involved and the themes dealt with. The most important theme is that of man's dual nature: we are all Lazaruses, with evil and goodness as constituents of our personality. And, it is implied, just as Lazarus had to come to grips with his evil nature, we must come to grips with ours, otherwise our world and our moral being will be annihilated. If we cannot do good, at least we can prevent ourselves from doing evil. We must, then, find a way of reconciling conflicting components of our personality; hopefully our goodness will triumph, though we cannot be certain of this.

This split between alternative selves is related to the problem we find symbolized by Mr. Spock—that of the man who fears that he cannot let himself go, cannot dare to feel, lest his evil nature be released and annihilate him. We are dealing with a theme that was brilliantly characterized in Stevenson's *Dr. Jekyll and Mr. Hyde*. As Martin Grotjahn says in *Beyond Laughter*:

> We live in constant dread that our unconscious may find its way to consciousness and overwhelm our controls: then Mr. Hyde would overpower Dr. Jekyll and would do all the bad things we had hoped were safely repressed a long time ago.

In the episode we have been discussing these alternative selves were given form in the two Lazaruses, but the message is clear: we all have two natures and we must resolve the conflict between them in order to survive and maintain our sanity. The alternatives we face are a kind of schizophrenia or a deadened, emotionless, mummylike existence.

There is also a social theme in this episode, as well as

a psychological one. I am talking about the notion of invasion, of the infection of the paradisical society by foreign elements. The starship *Enterprise* can be seen as a Utopian social and political community. It is racially and sexually integrated and international, a perfectly functioning social order. As it soars through the outer limits of space it is continually subjected to attempts by various entities, forces, beings and such to enter and take control of it, for a multitude of nefarious reasons.

The members of the crew represent, symbolically, a rather idealized picture of the typical American—clean-cut, efficient, courageous, and somewhat mechanical. They are portrayed pressing buttons, reading dials, manipulating gadgets, and almost as appendages to their marvelous machines. It is almost a parody of contemporary American society, full of clean-cut, semimechanical functionaries. The individuals are all good democrats, but the system is quasi-totalitarian, though that is to be expected in a military ambience. This smoothly functioning society is penetrated by some force, evil or good, and some kind of a solution is found in which the foreign elements are controlled, one way or another. The *Enterprise,* as a system, resists contamination and flies on to new adventures.

This theme is a central organizing myth in the American imagination. We have traditionally seen ourselves as Adamic innocents in a garden and have defined ourselves as non-Europeans, non-Asians, people who have escaped from history. History, in our mind, is identified with institutions, such as the Roman Catholic Church, royalty, a professional military caste, and so forth. This phenomenon was described by R. W. B. Lewis in *The American Adam,*

which discussed the American mind of the mid-nineteenth century:

> The new habits to be engendered on the new American scene were suggested by the image of a radically new personality, the hero of the new adventure: an individual emancipated from history, happily bereft of ancestry, untouched and undefiled by the usual inheritances of family and race; an individual standing alone, self-reliant and self-propelling, ready to confront whatever awaited him with the aid of his own, unique and inherent resources. It was not surprising, in a Bible-reading generation, that the new hero (in praise or disapproval) was most easily identified with Adam before the Fall. Adam was the first, the archetypal, man. His moral position was prior to experience, and in his very newness he was fundamentally innocent.

Given the belief that we were new Adams in a New Eden, our fundamental task is evident: we must keep the new Eden innocent, we must protect it from contamination . . . either by foreign bodies (immigrants) or foreign ideas (Catholicism, and Marxism, for example) and, we must maintain our own innocence.

Thus the adventures on *Star Trek* reflect this fundamental belief that we must maintain our innocence and protect ourselves from foreign influences. Ultimately we find man in a state of siege: he cannot allow that which is in him to escape, lest his aggressive impulses destroy those whom he loves (to the extent that he can love), and he must be on eternal guard against invasion and contamination from forces outside him. We find, then, a diffuse social paranoia, in which the fear of contamination creates a sense

of danger from without, and a fear of danger from within. There is no place to turn.

Of course I have been dealing with extreme cases and with beliefs (in our Adamic innocence), which are unwarranted, though which have shaped our behavior. The fact that *Star Trek* is based upon a ritual reenactment of our central organizing myth means that it is still with us, though it is buried deep within our unconscious, and is camouflaged. It may even be that our need to preserve our innocence, on an individual basis, is what is behind our lack of affection and fear of our feelings. If that is the case, we must face the consequences of our innocence—rather our belief in our innocence—and find a more salutary myth around which to organize our lives.

The success of televised football is one of the marvels of the modern era. While football has always been popular—especially with college-educated people—it didn't replace baseball as the central sport in the American consciousness until television came along and carried the game into millions of homes. There seems to be little question that there is a relationship between the increased popularity of football and the spread of television.

A number of reasons can be cited to explain why. For one thing, football televises very well. A football field is much smaller than a baseball field, and, in addition, the action in football is limited to a small area of the field most of the time. Baseball is much more diffuse. Though the focus tends to be in the confrontation between the pitcher and the batter, a hit can go anywhere and action occurs in several different places at the same time.

Football is also much more of a spectacle and entertainment. There are pretty girls, there are marching bands, there is an electric tension in the fans filling the huge stadiums—and all of this comes across to the viewer. In contrast, baseball is a relatively chaste, low-key game, which does not generate the excitement football does; baseball has an essential purity about it and isn't interested in "flash" and extraneous elements. Love it or leave it for its own sake. Thus televised football is an entertainment package, which includes many elements extraneous to the game itself. This is not the case with baseball, which is structured so that nothing can interfere with the game as it moves onward. Baseball requires a long attention span, and in certain cases (tie games) can last hours and hours.

In a tie game in which the pitchers are dominant, a game can last 12 or 15 innings with very little action taking place. Of course baseball can generate excitement in certain

situations, but baseball finds itself faced by a tragic dilemma: the better a game is—in terms of pitching, certainly—the less action there is and the lower the score. Thus baseball is best when it is least, and while a 1-0 win in a pitching duel might satisfy zealots, such games do not satisfy crowds, who have increasingly taken their business elsewhere.

*What I am suggesting is that baseball and football have different personalities and that as our temperament and character have changed, baseball has now become an anachronism. It is football that reflects the cultural dynamics in contemporary America.* To see this in more detail, examine the following chart which compares the two sports.

### CULTURAL DYNAMICS OF FOOTBALL AND BASEBALL

| FOOTBALL | BASEBALL |
|---|---|
| urban | pastoral |
| "educated" players | country boys |
| time precious | time not important |
| specialized | general |
| body contact important | body contact minimal |
| team effort | individualistic |
| upsets critical | no upsets |
| vicarious excitement | relaxation |
| weekly | daily |
| spectacle: bands, cheerleaders, mascots | austerity |
| four quarters with intermission | nine innings uninterrupted flow |
| calculation and planning | little strategy |
| body a weapon | bat a weapon |
| small area played on | large area played on |
| Twentieth Century | Nineteenth Century |
| territorial | not territorial |

This chart shows the differences between the two sports in graphic form, and though in certain cases I have exaggerated the characteristics of each sport to make a point, I think it is obvious that there are fundamental differences.

Football is twentieth century and urban; it reflects the present-day world in which time is precious, specialization is rampant, and planning is critical. After each play in football there is a "conference," so to speak, in which experts determine the course of action to take—given the situation in which the team finds itself. There are "game plans," which indicate the general course of action, and there are "plays" on the field, so we find both strategy and tactics employed. This suggests an analogy with war, and some have described football as a functional alternative or equivalent to war; that is, it enables us to have the same satisfactions we gain in battle, but with less cost. The football field, to carry the analogy further, represents a battlefield in which two armies contest for territory and try to achieve certain goals. In football, however, the battle is staged and the violence is subordinated to other aspects of the contest.

Football is also much closer to the medieval tournament, and has more spectacle than baseball. A football game is an entertainment. There are beautiful, scantily dressed, young girls leading cheers and jumping about; there are precision marching bands that seem to be made of robots; and there are baton twirlers, drum majors, mascots —all kinds of people who provide entertainment at a typical game.

The cheerleaders can be seen as modern equivalents of the "vestal virgins" in Roman gladiatorial combats, or of the "ladies" in tournament in medieval days. The cheer-

leaders are there to lead the crowd in chanting and cheering and also, I assume, to inspire the players. (The all-American football hero and the cheerleader are commonly linked in the popular imagination, just as the knight and the lady were in medieval days. Then as now, beauty is a reward for heroism.) The cheerleaders are young and attractive and provide some excellent girl-watching for viewers, to further extend the erotic element of the game. In addition there are the drum majorettes, though their function is slightly different. According to Marshall McLuhan (in *The Mechanical Bride*) the drum-majorette is a strange combination of "adolescent love novice" and flagellation symbol, a nymphet chorus girl in "cavalry officer" dress.

McLuhan cannot make sense of her and concludes that she is a "cluster image" that "represents a crude, garish and ludicrous hotch-potch of irreconcilable desires and imbecile motives. . . ." Even if there is little logic to the majorette, she is, obviously, what would now be called "a sexual object," like her sisters, the cheerleaders. The problem with the majorette is that she is a combination of two opposing elements, military order and precision and also sexuality. She may be one of the first manifestations of the *unisex* phenomenon; an important (noteworthy) desexualized figure who appeared in the 1920's and has been of considerable influence, to this day. (The miniskirted girl with high boots may be a modern but slightly camouflaged manifestation of the majorette.)

Structurally speaking there is an interesting opposition between the majorette and the marching band, who stand for precision, and the football players, who represent randomness and dance. Football involves a confrontation

between planning, rationality, and order, on the one hand, and accident, imagination, and initiative on the other hand. The members of the band and even the majorettes are anonymous robotlike figures, while the best players are all individuals, whose distinctive traits of personality (and whose neurotic afflictions) are well known to all followers of the game.

The language of football is violent, and is related to the notion of containing and avoiding containment, of dominating and refusing to be dominated. That is the central tension around which the game revolves. Thus we find quarterbacks who stay in the "pocket" and others who "roll out." Such terms as "smash," "hurdle," "hit," "block," "break tackle," "pop," involve the notion of breaking something up, preventing something from happening, and that kind of thing. The plays, which are called from the field or sent in by the coach, are all battle plans that involve specific and precise acts on the part of each member of each team.* The defensive team calls plays that will enable it to anticipate what the offense will do and prevent the offense from carrying out its plans. The defense in football is much more active and involved than in baseball.

Baseball is a nineteenth-century pastoral form, which involves country boys running around on grass and having a good time for themselves. The inexorable march of the clock is not critical in baseball, because time is not precious. The players are not specialists as in football; people are associated with a particular position in each game, but aside from pitchers, many players can (if necessary) play in other

---

* The fact that plays seldom work perfectly is a testimonial to man's incapacity to be turned into an automaton despite training camp, which is a kind of brainwashing. The marching band, however, suggests he can.

positions. In football the team is made of superspecialists and experts: one man only "runs the ball back" after punts and kickoffs, one player is a kicking specialist, players are defensive guards and not offensive guards, and so on— especially in professional football, which represents the complete rationalization of game into limited spheres.

In baseball there are generalists, who keep their eye on the ball and see the big picture; football is full of spec- ial-duty characters who are very limited in terms of their range but have depth. Baseball represents America before the frontier ended, when there was plenty of space and plenty of time, and philosophic anarchists roamed around in verdant fields "doing their thing" with a free and reckless abandon. The game is relaxing and not particularly taxing on the players, who play many times each week. Football is tremendously difficult on the players and is so tiring that sixty minutes of clock time—which amounts to several hours of real time—exhausts them. Baseball developed when we thought nature was a limitless reservoir and we would always live in abundance. Football reflects a different world view; everything has to be fought for, resources are pre- cious, hostile people (guards, monster men) are everywhere and in such a world you have to grab what you can.

In baseball a man swings a stick at a ball; in football (ignorant) armies clash—by day and by night.

The thrust of my argument, to this point, has been that football televises better than baseball and that football approximates the cultural dynamics of contemporary American society more closely than baseball does. The hard- pressed, urban, temporally directed American is now too hopped up for baseball; he doesn't get kicks from baseball —it bores him. Yet football has a rather mechanical quality

that can quickly become tedious. What saves football is the fact that there is such randomness in the rewards. At any given moment a sensational play is possible, and the fact that we cannot predict when the excitement will come means we must pay attention all the time.

With the invention of "instant replay," television football became different from live-action football. Television football is a combination of *Rashomon* and *Last Year at Marienbad*. The past keeps on repeating itself and life takes on a surrealistic quality, as the instant replay serves as a flashback into the past. In addition, you can see the same play from two or three different perspectives, and frequently, in the case of controversial calls by the referees, a play will be repeated three of four times. *Rashomon,* the classic Japanese film, dealt with the problem of knowing truth. Four different versions of an event were given in the film—three by the participants and one by an onlooker, yet there were reasons to doubt each and every description. Televised football deals with the same problem. It gives us different perspectives, from different cameras, of a controversial play and lets us make up our minds as to what happened. Or it merely presents a play in two or three versions, each of which gives a different picture and all of which together show us that reality is multiform.

Thanks to instant replay we are able to reconstruct the world, to interrupt the flow of time at a whim, and salvage passing moments. Time does not flow evenly but jumps around and the past can repeat itself over and over again. On the field the players are able to "stop" time and use it for their purposes; an incredible number of games are won and lost during the final minutes and seconds of a game. But the television producers are able to capture

time and bring it back to us; we no longer have to count on remembrances of things past. The control room conjures it up for us. Thus there is a tension established for the viewer between real time (on the field) and psychological time (on the television set). Football, on the field, is a game; on the screen it has become an art form.

★ **do big boys play cowboys and indians?**

The stereotyped Wild West story is perhaps the most significant contribution of Hollywood to the art form of movies and television. It is a contemporary variation of the ageless Oedipus theme. The hero is not the tragic Oedipus but the victorious son and brother. He is not the guilt-ridden, tragic figure who committed the crime, driven by the Erinyes of his unconscious underworld. In the Wild West drama, the hero is guiltless and the crime disguised. He avoids his tragic destiny. He behaves like Prometheus, who escaped with the stolen fire and avoided his punishment. The cowboy enacts a dream of glory which was dreamt through childhood and puberty. His adventures are enjoyed by the adolescent in us who is not willing to stop juvenile day-dreams. . . . The cowboy is a good son whose pseudo-rebellion serves the good of the father after

**145**

all. Therefore he goes on to repeat his adventure instead of settling his unconscious conflict.

—MARTIN GROTJAHN,
*Beyond Laughter*

The statistics about Westerns on television (and in the films, too) are simply remarkable. *Gunsmoke,* perhaps the greatest television Western, was first aired in 1955. At the height of its popularity, *Bonanza* was the most widely viewed television program in the world, and was broadcast in sixty different countries. During the peak years of 1958–1960, there were twenty-two different Western series on television according to Russell Nye in *The Unembarrassed Muse.* Though there are few television Westerns made now, between the movies and the reruns, it is possible to keep the most ardent fan of the Western happy with a plentiful supply of this genre.

*The problem of the Western is why it is so popular and what it tells us about American character and culture.* It is, after all, a distinctive American idiom, along with the comic strip, and though it is possible to make Westerns elsewhere (in Italy or Japan, for example), the Western is something that remains, for various reasons, quintessentially American. One reason for this is because it is, as its name suggests, tied to a particular location—the American West.

It is also associated with a particular period in American history—the last half of the nineteenth century when the frontier had not yet ended and the American West was not yet completely settled. It is both the period and the place that make possible the classical Western, and because other cultures do not have *both* of these ingredients, the

Western is native and uniquely American. The Japanese may have figures who are similar in certain ways—the samurai—but the setting is different; the samurai is rooted in history and the cowboy is rooted *outside* of it. Americans have traditionally defined themselves as existing beyond civilization, history, and institutions, and living in nature. It is the cowboy who represents this idealized picture of ourselves most clearly. He must mediate between the chaos of lawlessness and the tyranny of institutions and civilization (as represented best by Europe with its kings and cathedrals and castes).

The secret of America is that we have, so we believe, created our own natural institutions and home-grown remedies for the problems any collectivity faces. Russell Nye's description of *Gunsmoke* as a classical Western gives us some perspective here. He tells us that the program "embodies the classic Western theme of conflict between frontier and civilization" and deals with a city, Dodge City, that is endangered from within (by subversion) and from without (by hostile forces). Generally speaking the dangers are averted.

*The classical American problem is that of creating a natural community (a contradiction in terms, in truth), and the way we have done this is by defining society as an abstraction, which stands for a multitude of individuals each pursuing his private destiny.* The links between people are tenuous: they live in the same territory and have certain rights to be protected, but few have any sense of solidarity with their neighbors and there is little in the way of social consciousness—until, that is, a threat arises.

In a sense, it can be argued that the cowboy is an adolescent figure who appeared at a time when American

society was, itself, in the process of formation. We were moving from savagery to civilization and found ourselves in between these two stages. It is only logical, then, that a hero who arises in this period of instability would, himself, be unstable and lack a firm and coherent identity. The cowboy as mythic hero has a great sense of possibility and a well-defined *image*, thanks to his clothes, horse, six-shooters, and other paraphernalia. But like all adolescents he is continually searching for something; he is easily angered and prone to demonstrating his masculinity (via that metal phallus the sex- or six-shooter); and he thirsts for adventure. He searches for love which, being immature, he cannot accept, and he searches for a father figure, to emulate. He is capable of great heroism and great renunciations.

Quite likely it is the distinctiveness of his *image* that appeals to so many people, because he is, at least outwardly, wonderfully well defined. To anonymous and depersonalized people living in a bureaucratic mass society, the cowboy has obvious appeal. But as a person he is not integrated and that, in fact, may be the secret reason for his popularity. He is not rooted or trapped and is the captive only of his own psychological and moral imperatives. Perhaps it is the openness and inchoateness of the West that is what really fascinates us, for in a frontier ambience we feel a man can somehow create himself, a man has possibilities. And wandering through the West, through the phantasmagoria of Indians, cowboys in white linen, killers in black, telegraph operators, schoolmarms, saloon keepers, rustlers, sheriffs, are all kinds of people pursuing their dreams and fantasies, searching for opportunities, and above all, searching for some kind of a resolution to the tension within.

This notion about the significance of the Western in

relation to the problem of adolescence is held by others, though it is not the dominant interpretation of the Western. For example, in *The Six-Gun Mystique,* John Cawelti says:

> Since we have already noted the special connection between the Western formula and adolescent readers and movie-goers, this is probably the best place to begin a discussion of the ticklish subject of the Western as dream. If we accept Freud's conception of the dream as an expression in symbolism of unresolved conflicts between latent impulses and the attitudes of the conscious self we can at least suggest a tentative interpretation of the Western from the perspective of its relevance to the cultural situation of adolescents. From this point of view I suggest that the Western expresses the conflict between the adolescent's desire to be an adult and his fear and hesitation about the nature of adulthood.

We must not be misled by the fact that many of the heroes of Westerns are not particularly youthful figures, for it is not age but psychological development we are talking about. We must also remember that the notion that youth is morally superior to adults and must teach and save adults is a common theme in our popular culture.

The dilemma an American faces is that, having renounced history, his fatherland (and perhaps his real father) and the past, having set out for the new territories where there was freedom and opportunity, he now discovers no suitable role model to imitate and he is locked into a perpetual adolescence, doomed to search for a useable self and destined never to grow up. Is it any wonder, then, that America is full of thirty- and forty-year old "kids" now? When we abandoned the old world and history and structure, we

also abandoned rituals which would confirm identity through rites of initiation indicating how we were progressing toward an adult status. Everyone was thrown upon his own devices. The result was psychic chaos and it still is; though they do not recognize it, people who stage identity voyages by dressing "western" are building identities upon shifting sands. We may even ask ourselves whether the "law and order" with which Westerns concern themselves is only the outward, social manifestation of a struggle that is being waged intrapsychically within the typical Western hero.

I have been discussing the Western on a very high level of abstraction. There is something about the subject that lends itself to this kind of treatment. If Westerns involve, among other things, moral crises over the need to use violence (in their most classical manifestations), then there is almost an invitation to write in a somewhat philosophical manner. The very notion of a moral crisis suggests the hero of the Western finds himself torn between opposing forces and finds it is his duty to solve them, one way or another. (I have dealt with this subject in my chapter on *Kung Fu,* which is also involved with Western themes.) I would like to turn now to an episode from *Gunsmoke,* which shows oppositions and their resolutions with great clarity. I might say that I found this particular program quite moving, though I felt the ending was somewhat sentimental.

This episode was called "And I Have Promises to Keep," and dealt with the efforts of a minister from the East to build a church and preach to the Indians in the West. The only figure from the *Gunsmoke* cast who has a significant part in the program is Festus. He is in another

town taking care of some business when he becomes involved in an argument between the minister and the local lumber dealer, who doesn't want to sell the minister lumber. Festus becomes implicated more and more deeply, and eventually decides to accompany the minister to the location where he is to build the church. He discovers that the minister doesn't know how to build anything, and stays on to construct the building. Late one evening the townsfolk come and burn down the frame that the minister and Festus have constructed. The minister wants to give up, feeling guilty about having stirred up such hatred, but Festus is not deterred and insists that they continue on with the project.

Festus then goes into town, interrupts a Sunday service in the church to chastize the people in the town for being hypocrites and treading on the dream of the minister from the East, and returns to help with the church. He also goes to the Indians to ask them to come, just once, to hear the minister preach. The Indians refuse, saying: "We want to keep on to our old ways." Festus gives them his horse, to show the depths of his feelings, hoping this will move the Indians to attend services. They do attend, and in the middle of the services the minister has a heart attack and dies. The Indians give Festus back his horse, and, as the program ends, the townsfolk are bringing lumber to complete the church, and the minister from the town decides to continue on with the work of preaching to the Indians. He has had a change of heart, after having been criticized by the Eastern minister for "sanctifying the prejudices and hatreds of the townsfolk" as far as the Indians were concerned.

This capsule description of the plot does not do justice

to the program, which was beautifully acted and very well written. It had a dramatic integrity to it that made it a powerful and moving experience. What I am concerned with here is not so much the plot of the episode but rather the structural oppositions that underlay the program and gave it such remarkable cultural resonance. What we find is that there are a series of oppositions here; it is not a simple matter of the "good guys" against the "bad guys," and it may be this matter of multiple oppositions that is distinctive to the adult and sophisticated Western (or adult program of any genre).

First, let us contrast Festus and the Eastern minister.

| FESTUS | EASTERN MINISTER |
|---|---|
| natural man | urban, sophisticated man |
| illiterate | educated |
| shrewd | naïve |
| practical | impractical |
| easy-going, relaxed | driven (must preach to Indians) |

These are the common attributes, respectively, of the Western "natural" man and the Eastern "civilized" man, as our popular imagination saw things in the mid-nineteenth century, and these cultural stereotypes are still with us to this day, though, in modified and camouflaged forms.

What united Festus and the minister is a sense of decency and humanity and great moral courage. The minister had retired, forsaken an easy and comfortable (but spiritually unrewarding) ministry in the East; he came to the West to fulfill his vocation. Festus becomes implicated and realizes that *he* must save the would-be savior, who is out of his element in the West. We recognize that the minis-

ter's faith is powerful and, in effect, has brought Festus to him as his redeemer.

There are other oppositions to be made in this story:

| | |
|---|---|
| the Eastern minister with his mission to the Indians | the town minister who is living comfortably and sanctifying prejudices |
| the Indians who fear and hate the Townsfolk | the townsfolk who fear and hate the Indians |
| the Eastern minister's desire to convert the Indians | the Indians' desire to maintain their cultural heritage, to keep their old ways |
| Festus, who decides to help the Eastern minister | the townsfolk, who oppose the Eastern minister |

This listing suggests that the oppositions do not line up simply in terms of good versus bad, for it is quite likely that the Indians are right in their desire to maintain their old ways and hold on to their heritage. We are told, also, that the townsfolk have reason to be bitter about the Indians, since there were bloody wars, which just ended a few years back. Thus we find ourselves in a very complex situation, from a moral point of view.

There is even a suggestion that the Eastern minister is pursuing a somewhat mad and destructive course. There is a scene in which we find him reading *Moby Dick,* and telling Festus about Ahab and his tormented pursuit of the white whale. Both pursuits will, it is implied, end in victory and self-destruction. What was significant in this

episode, in terms of American values and culture, was the strength and courageousness of Festus, the "natural" man, (so natural, in fact, that he cannot even read). He finds himself caught between opposing forces and finds a way to mediate between them. The Eastern minister must be allowed to pursue his dream and the town minister must be shaken from his spiritual lethargy. The hatred between the townsfolk and the Indians must be stopped and reparations made. The oppositions must be resolved in some manner so people can live together in harmony, and also live with themselves. For we must rid ourselves of hatred lest we destroy ourselves by hating the hatred *within* ourselves.

There is, I believe, a parallel between the problems the *cowboy,* as adolescent, faces and those the lawless, prepolitical town faces: both must solve the dilemma of dissociateness, both must achieve some kind of a unity, despite forces pulling each in various directions. Long ago Freud pointed out that infants have sexual drives, but that they are dissociated; and it is only in adulthood that they become focused and, hence, evident. *The cowboy as adolescent must solve the questions of sex and self to achieve adulthood and a distinctive identity, and the town must solve the problem of anarchy and lawlessness to become a community.* These problems and their resolution are diagrammed below:

| FIGURE/ENTITY | LEVEL | PROBLEM | | RESOLUTION |
|---|---|---|---|---|
| cowboy | personal | adolescent | sex | adulthood |
| | | | self | (unification) |
| town | social | anarchy | society | community |
| | | | | (order) |

Thus there is a reciprocity between the individual and his social milieu in the Western that we do not find, for example, in the detective story—where society is already defined and highly organized.

The Western appeals to us because it is prepolitical and prebureaucratic; it is an empty vessel of *potentiality* into which we can pour an infinite number of different plots, mythic heroes, character types, settings, stereotypes, themes, and so forth. We can still dream about creativity in nature and the possibility of establishing our own "natural" institutions. That dream has faded and we now see ourselves as prisoners, hostages of an overwhelming and de-individuating urban environment in which the goal is not so much self-creation but survival. Our heroes are now characters like Colombo and Chief Ironside and Kojak; they are bureaucrats who hunt criminals and preserve the public order.

Perhaps the demise of the Western as a dominant form of popular art symbolizes the ultimate loss of innocence in the American public, and our loss of belief in each person's capacity to create himself. Illiterates like Festus are no longer tutelary figures for educated but helpless persons (or parsons), and the heroes of the modern day are civil servants in and out of police uniforms.

The police procedurals may be more in keeping with the outward and most obvious aspects of contemporary American society, but I do not think they capture the psychological imperatives that released such great energy in this country. Cops and robbers may be more modern than cowboys and Indians, but as any little kid can tell you, it isn't necessarily more satisfying.

★ **or the law of the excluded middle**

Americans have long defined themselves as middle class. We believe we have a classless middle-class society, with small fringes of people on either side—the fabulously wealthy and the desperately poor—but they are anachronisms and, ineluctably, everyone will be middle class in America. From this point of view, to be an American involves not only being open to experience, but also resigned to the comforts of bourgeois life. After all, we have no hereditary aristocracy, like the British, and we never had feudalism in America, so habits of deference and the belief that some people are better than others are foreign to us.

In recent years we have come to recognize that the poor are more numerous and more desperate than we

156

thought they were, but since what they want (as riots suggest) are cars and color television sets, we can rest assured that they have the souls of the middle class, if not their fat wallets. We have also discovered the rich have been around longer than we thought, and may be some kind of a non-titled ruling class.

But our ruling classes are also essentially bourgeois, and besides, our basic myth is that we can rise to the top, so we've not been too hard on them. Otherwise, we fear, they won't let us into the club. The diffuse sense of class-lessness has its drawback, however; it leads to a great deal of anxiety and restlessness. Since we never can be sure where we are on the social scale, we don't know how to act and what is proper, hence the dilemmas of conforming individualists in America.

That is why *Upstairs-Downstairs* is so comforting to Americans. We are so involved with being "masterless" men that it is a relief to see people who know precisely who they are and what they can expect out of life. *Upstairs-Downstairs* is really a high-toned soap opera. According to the *Random House Dictionary* (The Unabridged Edition) a soap opera is

> a serialized program presented on radio or television dramatizing the personal and domestic problems or a fictional character, family, or group in a sentimental, melodramatic way—[so called from the fact that many such programs were sponsored by soap companies].

It does not have the hysterics, the brain operations, and the absurdity of the typical American soap opera, but it has the structure, except that each episode in *Upstairs-Downstairs* is complete in itself.

The world of *Upstairs-Downstairs* is the world of two discrete classes—the wealthy and the poor, the masters and their servants. It is very binary, reducing English society to its two extremes and presenting what is essentially a middle-class*less* point of view. A society that is all center, so to speak, can watch a program about a society that has no center—at least as we see things. Perhaps Americans, who are feverishly upward-mobile, take a kind of pleasure in seeing people who never think about such things . . . or at least never seem to. Everyone seems to have his place in the Great Chain of Being and is reconciled to it. How charmingly medieval, but then it takes place in the second decade of the 1900's, in England.

I would like to explore the differences between the two classes presented in more detail, and the following chart portrays the contrasting points of view of the people who live upstairs and downstairs:

| UPSTAIRS | DOWNSTAIRS |
|---|---|
| wealthy | poor |
| masters (command) | servants (obey) |
| educated (but often silly) | not educated (but often shrewd) |
| leisure | hard work |
| openness | closure |
| space | crowdedness |
| champagne | beer |
| marriage and infidelity | bachelorhood and spinsterhood |

Although they have different perspectives and inhabit different worlds, for all practical purposes, the relations between the masters and servants are dignified and proper, on all

sides. There is respect all around and the servants all have an essential dignity that is admirable. That is the irony of it all, as far as Americans are concerned. We are all master-less men who serve no one, but we feel a strong sense of alienation and de-individuation. Because we respect no-body, nobody respects us, and our supposed freedom seems to offer little except isolation.

It may be because identity in America is so much in-volved with negation, with being men and women with no categories. How curious it is that the English working classes, hemmed in and without the sense of possibility that American middle-class people have, seem to be so beauti-fully defined, seem to have so much identity. It is almost as if the chains that bind them (in our view of things) support them, also. Thus an Englishman like Hudson, the butler, exudes a kind of security and strength that we cannot help but admire. The average middle-class American identifies with the people upstairs, obviously, but he doesn't really have their style nor their real possibilities, and most cer-tainly he doesn't have their manners.

The most fundamental theme in the series is that of the difference between the wealthy and the poor "service" class, and we see this in almost very episode. The superior-ity of the wealthy does not extend to the realm of morality, and we find frequent examples of the narrowness and triviality of those who are wealthy. They are portrayed (and I am thinking of the episode in which Hudson and Captain James Bellamy go off to a country weekend) as bored, infan-tile, and venal. It is the servants who hold their lives to-gether, just as it is the working classes who are exploited and create the vast wealth, which the rich squander. A Jewish businessman confides to Captain James, as they

observe the goings-on at the country house both are visiting, he would put a gun to his head rather than lead the empty life that was typical of this class. And yet, for all their frivolity and lassitude, the young men had a sense of duty and honor that was commendable, as the episode about the coming of the First World War showed. They did not recognize the immensity of the forces at work, but they bravely raced in to do their duty.

They ran off to war as if it were a continuation of their garden party, but for people whose lives were garden parties, such is to be expected. What is curious to me, and I have recently spent a year in England, is that there is still the same ambience in London that we find in *Upstairs-Downstairs*. What I am talking about basically is the sense of closure that still permeates the atmosphere; true, the working classes have had many advances and England is now a democratic socialist state, but in a rather curious way, England seems as binary as *Upstair-Downstairs* would suggest it was. Class distinctions are still very strong and the notion of order and hierarchy is all-pervasive, though there is now a sizeable middle class. I came away with the feeling that England is still a working-class nation controlled by a small and generally very rich upper class.

Just as in *Upstairs-Downstairs,* this upper class, the people "upstairs," have given the masses security; that is, after all, what is most important to the working classes and the people "downstairs." In one episode, when the household seems on the verge of disintegration, and Captain James is not sleeping with his wife, Hazel, anymore, fighting and disarray break out among the servants. As Daisy, the maid says, "I don't feel safe anymore." Though the servants "downstairs" are separated from the masters

"upstairs," their lives are very obviously connected. The title of the series emphasizes social distance, but though the house must be, as Captain James tells Hazel, "run with dignity from upstairs," the lives of everyone are merged together. The moral of this is that when the rulers lose their grasp of things, chaos and disarray can be expected from the masses.

The Bellamy household is obviously a microcosm, which represents a macrocosm, that is, England itself. The marriage of Edward Bellamy's son James to Hazel, Edward's former typist, takes on, then, a symbolic significance. James has married beneath him and the essential clarity that had characterized all relations betwen the two classes are now clouded. When those "upstairs" and those "downstairs" maintained proper relations, based upon respect and deference, England was sure of itself and life was harmonious. When the essential simplicity of the situation was destroyed, the stage was set for tumult and chaos.

The fearful and conservative elements in the working classes, Hudson for example, feared for the worst. Hudson believed that James had made a great mistake in marrying Hazel and blamed her for all the trouble the household was experiencing. Rose, on the other hand, disagreed and told Hudson he was living in the past. "She had the chance," Rose said, "and she took it." The immediate cause of the difficulties was the miscarriage of Hazel, which drove James from her. On the personal level it reflects his basically infantile personality; she had deprived him of a toy, which he wanted, and this led him to turn his attention elsewhere. On the cultural level, it may mean that James, as one of the ruling classes, recognized that he had made a fatal error: the bloodline was contaminated, the progeny would

either not exist, or certainly not be the same. When "downstairs" sleeps with "upstairs" on the marriage bed, something incredible has happened and the old way is doomed. The story of James and Hazel is a parable about the dissolution of the English way of life at the period just before the First World War. The changes that have taken place in England have been profound, though as I said I still have the impression that there is a great deal of class distinction remaining in England.

One of the reasons for the popularity of the series here is that it is so beautifully acted. The cast is extraordinary and there is hardly ever a false note to be found in any episode, a tribute to the writers at the ITV broadcasting corporation. They seem to have a genius for turning out fascinating series of programs, which have the priceless quality of being adult and which hook you and draw you into them, until you feel you must keep up and watch each and every episode. This is only possible because we are curious, but if our curiosity were not whetted by interesting material, we would not become so involved.

In the case of *Upstairs-Downstairs*—as in the case of *Kung Fu*—we find the controlling matter to be the resolution of the dialectic, which is central to the series.

Characters find themselves in all kinds of situations, people fall in and out of love, there are personal tragedies and social cataclysms, but pervading everything are the two classes, the oppositions, which form a kind of ground or background against which figures play out their lives. In America we have resolved the dialectic, for better or worse, and we are curious about England—or, to be more precise, the United Kingdom. We have, we believe, escaped from history and in so doing escaped from domination by people

"upstairs." For all practical purposes, we are in between the two domains and have expanded our stake on the stairway until it dominates our house. But we still have notions that life upstairs may be more interesting and have our eyes turned in that direction. While we ponder the future and the dialectic, one thing seems certain: it is useful knowing how to type.

## ★ what TV tells us about ourselves

Culture is not merely a common code or even a common catalogue of answers to recurring problems; it is a common set of previously assimilated master patterns from which, by an "art of invention" similar to that involved in the writing of music, an infinite number of individual patterns directly applicable to specific situations are generated. The *topoi* [topics] are not only commonplaces but also patterns of invention and supports for improvisation.

—PIERRE BOURDIEU,
    "Systems of Education and
    Systems of Thought"

### Benny Hill

It is a commonplace that comedians tell a great deal about

**164**

the society in which they are found. They have a tendency to latch on to a society's embarrassments, to poke fun and ridicule the central figures of authority and point out (often without realizing it) the preoccupations of the man in the street. Humor is, then, national as well as international, and certain kinds of humor appeal to certain classes with certain levels of education, tastes, values, and beliefs. Some comedians transcend the boundaries of state and class and ethnicity, but most do not; some comedians are tied very directly to the tastes and attitudes of their audience and these comedians are very useful to anyone probing a society.

Chaplin tells you about the human condition. Morecambe and Wise or "The Two Ronnies" or Benny Hill tell you a great deal about what makes Englishmen laugh, and when we know this we know a good deal about English culture and society.

Although Morecambe and Wise and "The Two Ronnies" are almost national institutions, *The Benny Hill Show* of December 5, 1973, got the highest ratings of any show that week, and I would like to describe it in detail (and another of his shows) as a means toward characterizing English humor.

The show started out with Benny in drag, satirizing a Saran Wrap commercial. He was demonstrating how the wrap stuck to the sides of a glass, and "inadverently" poured a glass of milk over him/herself. Next came a funny song, in which he mocked some of the conventions of English culture. This was followed by a satire of a championship snooker match. In this skit a woman with large and scantily covered breasts flirts with him and distracts him and he loses the match. She then turns out to be the wife

of his opponent. This was followed by a skit in which he is a German selling clothes. He speaks with a German accent and talks about "titzen" and says at one point, "What nature has forgotten we supply with cotton."

In the next skit he is shown at the movies, seated between two sexy women. He acts out the roles shown on the screen, and in the process does crude things like picking his nose. This was followed by some short cameos in which he impersonated women, made sex gags, and did other bits. One skit showed a room full of people who had committed suicide in various ways. The radio in the room blared forth, "You have just heard the Prime Minister's address on the state of the nation. . . ."

Next came a spoof of phone-in shows. A cabinet officer, one Humphrey Bumphrey, was on talking about food, and making comments about people who "wee-weed all the way home" and men whose wives made their "peanut" brittle.

A "censored ad" came next, which featured a buxom girl with much cleavage showing, attacking a man at a concert. The program ended with a comic bandstand concert, which involved all kinds of strange things related to it and the park in which it was being held. A gardener watering the flowers seemed to be peeing. There was a spoof of bullfighting by a man and his crew picking up papers. Someone was involved in a situation in which he accidentally felt a girl's breasts. And there was a marvelously comic Apache dance.

Another *Benny Hill Show,* which came on December 27, 1973, was similar to the first. It had a large number of skits, poked fun at embarrassing aspects of English culture (the trials then underway of various call girls and their sex orgies with members of the BBC), and had a good deal of

gross word play about peeing, cockells, and so forth. There was a comic song: "Give me an older woman every time— they don't yell, they don't tell, and they are grateful as hell." The program closed with a brilliant series of skits, which were variations on the theme of Little Bo Peep. The tale was told as a Swedish sex film (*Naked Lust in Sweden*), as a news program, as a Shakesperian monologue starring a mock Lawrence Olivier, and as an Ironsides detective drama.

Hill is not perfectly representative, but his shows do provide us with most of the standard ploys of English mass humor, and his popularity suggests that he is worth considering. His programs (and I am generalizing from the two shows I've seen) are fascinating combinations of crudity and sophistication. Much of his humor—and he is typical in this respect—is terribly gross: language play about breasts and urinating and rear ends—what might be called "tit-piss" comedy, which is a combination of sex and sex-exhibitionism and bathroom humor. It is all quite infantile.

Yet, on the other hand, some of the skits are brilliantly conceived and acted, and the very notion of "a theme and variations" implies a somewhat sophisticated and complex view of reality. Hill makes superb use of film, and parts of his shows have a surrealistic quality.

Hill and his comic compeers suggest to me, first of all, that there is something mixed up in the English mind as far as sexuality is concerned. On a superficial level the English comics seem to be very direct about sex, and you see a good deal of cleavage in the girls who act in the various skits. But something seems amiss. The English seem to be breast fetishists (you see much more breast in England than

you do in America, generally speaking), yet they are quite crude about breasts, and the alliance with breasts and the bathroom reinforces my notion that the English are infantile and arrested in their sexual development. Perhaps they are mixed up somewhere in the oral-anal levels and have not moved on to the genital?

This may explain the great fondness English comics have for appearing as women. Someone suggested to me that Americans are so insecure about their masculinity that they cannot take the chance of appearing as women (even though their role as comics gives them liberties and even though they can be shown as quite obviously men pretending to be a women). You see a great deal more theatrical transvestism in England than you do in America, and I'm not certain that this is because the English are so secure in their sexual roles and their masculinity, that they can play women without being thought to be homosexuals.

The homosexual is also a standard comic figure here, and many shows have actors who play at being gay. This is a cheap laugh in America—just as word play about breasts and other parts of the anatomy is considered cheap. English mass humor is working-class humor and must appeal to working-class tastes—which are not, as a rule, very sophisticated. American mass humor is basically middle class—and to a large degree Jewish, as a result of the fact that an extraordinary number of comedians and comedy writers happen to be Jewish. American humor is therefore much more social and political and (for other reasons) much more *engaged,* much more critical. English humor is preoccupied with sexuality and bowel movements—a kind of primitive groping toward identity and maturity.

English humor does take occasional pot shots (or per-

haps potty shots) at the rich and the upper-class type; the individual with the received pronunciation is a comic figure here, but all of this is only illusion. The working classes resent the upper classes and take comfort in the portrayal of the upper classes as fools, but in reality it is the upper classes who have the last laugh, for they have the power and the wealth. The humor serves to dissipate anger and dissent in the working classes. The aggression is verbal and though it expresses resentment, it *does* nothing. This kind of humor does not really undermine the status quo, because it rails at a fantastic creation, a bogeyman who is by definition absurd.

English humor—the humor one finds on the television set—is generally, then, reactionary. Humor tends to be social and usually is a disguised attack on the status quo, but this is only possible when the humor has an outward reach. When the humor focuses on sex and body functions and patently absurd types, it is not and cannot be social or political. It is, in fact, to a great degree, a kind of premasturbatory, idiosyncratic fantasy, which confuses and confounds (sexuality identity becomes problematic with men as women and women as men), is privatistic and *unwittingly*—a word well chosen—supports the state and the status quo.

### Ronnie Corbett

Ronnie Corbett is the little man in the team of "The Two Ronnies." Along with Morecambe and Wise, the Two Ronnies are probably the top popular comedians of present-day England, and Ronnie Corbett, in fact, gave a performance along with a group of top stars for the queen recently. It was for some royal charity. He is a very short man and makes capital of this.

(I have frequently noticed that England is full of very short people. It might have something to do with the diet and a general undernourishment that has characterized the working classes there in the past, and perhaps even to this day.)

He frequently alludes to his shortness, and very often finds himself involved with beautiful and tall women. This means that he reaches, more or less, to their breasts, which are directly in his line of vision, and this situation is "milked" for laughs. He becomes, in such situations, a little boy—but a boy who knows much of the world. His face has a sly and knowing expressiveness. He has a worldly smirk—the kind you might find on a Puck, who realizes "what fools these mortals be," but also on the face of a lower-middle-class arriviste, who has made his way out of the squalor and slums into some kind of a good life.

Corbett is a superb actor; his face is expressive and he has a brilliant sense of timing. In one skit, shown around Christmas, 1973, he was involved with a tall, lovely young woman who was more or less foisted upon him by her mother. He engaged in a remarkable exercise in confusion by asking the woman whether she wanted to move from chair to chair, asking her what she wanted to drink, and suggesting alternately port and sherry, and harassing her until she left.

During this skit he was obviously very nervous and mixed up, and it seemed that the presence of this lovely woman was the source of his difficulties. He seemed to be embarrassed and unable to make up his mind or act logically, so that ultimatly he lost the girl, who got fed up with him and left the room. In fact, however, he was (it turned out) trying to get her to leave.

When she did leave he said, "At last!" Then he opened the top of a grand piano in the room, and helped out another young lady who may have been a maid—whereupon they embraced. They had obviously been interrupted in their lovemaking. The television audience, myself included, had been led astray. They had misjudged his motivations due to his actions—calculated to deceive the audience—and on the basis of their notions about how short men act when in the presence of tall and lovely women.

The acting was superb and the combination of a short, confused, perhaps "awed" lower-class man, who was also older, and a slender, refined, and beautiful young woman was obviously absurd.* He was not presented as a lower-class individual; in fact, Ronnie Corbett seems to delight in putting on finery and affecting rather obviously very smooth and self-assured upper-class types, but Ronnie as a "little man" and as a result of his undistinguished accent obviously comes across as someone from the middle classes, at best.

He represents the triumph of the little man, who, if he is shrewd and quick enough, can master the masters. He may seem to be out of his element at times, but he has a few tricks up his sleeve and frequently, in the final analysis, calls the tune.

### *Monty Python's Flying Circus!*

In the course of my research in England, I mentioned to a number of people that I was very much interested in English humor. Almost all of them have said something to

---

* In *Casino Royale* he also played a little man who was susceptible to the charms of tall and sexy women, though in this case there was an element of terror involved in his role.

this effect: "It's a pity Monty Python isn't on now. You really must see that show if you want to see something brilliant."

On Sunday, December 30, a replay of a Monty Python show was broadcast, which I looked forward to with considerable interpretation. Unfortunately I found it to be quite boring and not particularly funny. It started off as a spoof of an anthropological film, about the "migration" of people from Surbiton and Hunslow, and moved on to a lecture about Tchaikovsky held by a farming club, a play in which everyone wore "Trim Jeans" (hip slimmers), and other madcaps—including the sinking of the *Titanic*. __

There were occasional moments of hilarity and some tolerably good skits, but for the most part it was quite amateurish. *The Flying Circus's* "thing" obviously is absurdity and whackyness: famous people are caricatured, clichés are ridiculed, and the madness of English society is mirrored in a mad show. But the problem with *Monty Python's Flying Circus* is that it is too studied and, at the same time, poorly done. I got the feeling that the people in the show were having a grand time and a great deal of fun, but the show itself lacked finesse and real absurdity, except for an occasional bright spot.

What *The Flying Circus* fails to realize is that the *humor must do more than reflect the madness of a given society. That is the fallacy of imitative form. The function of the artist—and comic artists are included here—is to point out the madness and absurdity in a society by assuming some kind of a stance. The Circus* is full of crazies whose pose makes them forfeit all claim to seriousness. They do focus attention on some of the more absurd aspects of society, but they do not carry their criticism far enough.

The show has lots of flash, with modern graphics and

occasional animated sequences, and is generally amusing. I did not find it very funny or at all memorable. It also had too much sexual masquerading—men dressed as women, whose "little boys" turned out to be high-ranking government officials—and too much queer humor, in which an obviously homosexual man described as a hairdresser gave a brief synopsis of Tchaikovsky's life (though it might have been the gay's life. . . . I can't recall).

The show had no logic or structure to it, though it did have a certain amount of continuity. In fact, it was the element of continuity in the script that made me look for some kind of organization and for some kind of a satisfactory closure. The show, instead, seems to be open-ended, which is perfectly acceptable as long as the program makes no intimations of coherence. Probably the best word for *The Flying Circus* is *sophomoric.* It is a collection of gags, most rather banal, that don't add up to anything, and seems very much like the kind of thing students do in amateur theatricals in America, or camp counselors do when the staff has a variety show to put on.

Most English television humor is sophomoric. It is crude; it is obvious; it takes on easy marks (homosexuals); it has very little in the way of ideas; it is fascinated by body functions and not sure of itself about sexuality; and it isn't —as far as I am concerned, as an American—very funny. I also frequently detect a faint element of condescension in the arty, whacky, zany English comedy programs like Monty Python's, which are, purposefully, above the ordinary man.

There was one short scene in the Monty Python show that was brilliant. It only took a minute and was called "Fish Slapping Dance." In this skit two British soldiers stood on an embankment high over a river. One soldier

stood at attention while the other soldier slapped him with a little fish. After thirty seconds of this the soldier stopped slapping his colleague. The second soldier then took an enormous fish and slapped the first soldier, toppling him into the river.

This was funny for a number of reasons. First, the very notion of slapping someone with fish is quite absurd. It is an extraordinary conception and amuses us because it is so silly. It was called a dance, but obviously was not a dance —or not one that anyone in the audience (I presume) was familiar with—so on that level it also was comic. Especially since this was a dance in which nobody moved at all. There is also the element of slapstick about something like this. Slapping somebody with a fish is not far removed from pushing a pie in his face, but it is sufficiently removed to be original and entertaining. Finally, the element of surprise and amazement that came when the second soldier whipped out his enormous fish and clobbered the first soldier created a funny moment. It was really a dirty blow. You don't slap a person with an enormous fish. It became a club and the weight of the fish toppled the poor soldier and landed him in the drink. He exchanged places with the fish, who should have been in the water in the first place.

We find in this little scene a number of incongruities that are amusing, and which add up to a rather complicated (from an intellectual and analytical standpoint) matter. Generally speaking soldiers don't slap one another, and almost never with fish. When they do slap themselves with fish they should do so with fish of equal size and one soldier should not use a fish weighing a half a pound and another use one weighing thirty pounds. You don't dance by standing still, also.

This gag is an assault on your rationality and our sense of what is reasonable, and it is a bright spot in an otherwise undistinguished and mediocre program.

To sum it up, English mass humor is quite different from American humor, which may explain why English comedians are not, as a rule, successful here. Americans like sophisticated English humor, found in English films, but English popular humor involves different codes and is a reflection of a different culture. England and America really *are*, as the joke goes, two countries separated by a common language.

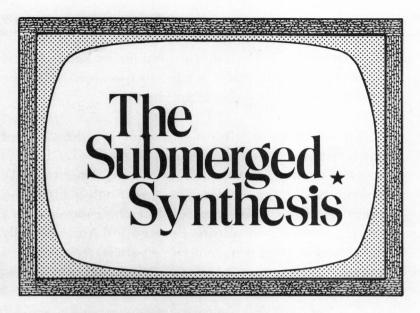

# The Submerged ★ Synthesis

## ★ or what makes Englishmen laugh?

I can't imagine that any reader will have agreed with *every-thing* I've had to say in this book, but that is to be expected. There is no reason anyone should like or agree with all my ideas; were anyone to find himself in that situation probably he would be terribly bored. *Why read about anything if you know it all yourself?* My advice to the reader is—take what you like and discard what you don't.

The average reader derives a good deal of pleasure from disagreeing with the printed word; it provides an opportunity for self-assertion in the face of the "authority" and finality of print. Some readers and critics enjoy ripping books to pieces, thereby demonstrating how brilliant *they*

are, thereby fending off what I imagine to be feelings of inadequacy and inconsequentiality. (This syndrome is particularly noticeable in academia in assistant professors, who tend to think they know it all, and obscure, anonymous full professors out to demonstrate they are diamonds in the rough.) People low down on the totem pole tend to be mean and to hold onto what little they have. Low-ranking officials and petty bureaucrats are not the best people to deal with, if you wish to get anything done.

If you don't want to think of this book as "social science" (whatever that may be), think of it as fiction. This book may be a new kind of autobiography. Hard-nosed scientists, looking for numbers and models and such, will be terribly disappointed and will have to make do with my psychoanalytical interpretations and references to such vagaries as national character and identity. This book may be what is frequently called "culture criticism" by sociologues. You, the reader, can make up your own mind. You can decide whether I've had anything interesting to say about the various programs I've analyzed and whether the essays make sense to you. Do they help, in any way, with your understanding yourself, your situation in the world, the problems you face? Do they give you any notions about why you watch certain television programs and what they may be doing for and to you?

There are various techniques that can be adopted in writing a book. Some authors take some hypothesis or generalization they wish to prove and look for material relative to their interest. For example, Charles Winick has taken the theme of desexualization and demonstrated in his book, *The New People*, how it informs almost every aspect of contemporary American culture. After examining desex-

ualization in American culture he came to certain chilling conclusions about what the future holds for us.

I tend to work the opposite way around. In this book, for example, I took television programs or media events that struck me as remarkable or significant, and analyzed each program as a discrete entity. I did the same thing with comics in my book, *The Comic-Stripped American*, and I believe it is a valid way of operating. Marshall McLuhan's *The Mechanical Bride* is organized in a similar manner, except that it focuses primarily on advertisements. While *The Mechanical Bride* is not "scientific" per se according to the basic most simplistic canons of social science, its suggestive power and resonance make it infinitely more valuable and important, I believe, than the greater part of the supposedly more rigorous work done in the social sciences.

For the fact is that we cannot measure *everything* and so those who believe only in measurement and statistical procedures measure only what is accessible to them, which may not necessarily be particularly important. The result is that work done in the social sciences is frequently reliable but trivial. The quest for certainty—which stems from our Puritan roots, according to Rollo May—has led to gross aberrations, and inquisitive sociologists have been replaced by sociological inquisitors. With the development of computers and other gadgets, the behaviorists have now gone mad, and have banished from their realm—or are trying to —social philosophers, social critics, philosophers, culture critics, and so forth. It is a sad story.

That last sentence is enough to incur the wrath of many social scientists who pride themselves on being "value free." To maintain this stance and still live in society, they divide themselves up into two halves: one half is their role

as value-free social scientist and the other is as ordinary human being and citizen. Were anyone interested in psycho-analytic matters to suggest this is a kind of schizophrenia, he would be labeled a crank by the value-free social scientist.

So my sentiments and sympathies are somewhat far removed from the mainstream of the sociological tradition, and people have, from time to time, suggested I am not *really* a social scientist. My answer is that if social science does not have room enough for a person like me, so much the worse for it.

This book, then, represents my interpretations, my analyses, my critiques of a selection of television programs, which I believe are worth looking at carefully. I brought no preconceived notions with me when I examined each program other than the belief that the individual program or series or both had a great deal of interesting material, and that a careful examination of television programs would reveal a great deal about our psyches and our culture.

As I indicated earlier, it is awesome, when you think about it, to write about television. There have been so many series, so many programs, so many specials, that I have been forced to neglect a great deal of material that is worth writing about. During any week in any decent-sized city there are hundreds and hundreds of programs: old movies, music programs, awards nights, roasts, quiz programs, soap operas, crime shows, sports events, documentaries—you name it. Dealing with television is Sisyphusian—there is no end to it, for new programs are being born all the time, and just when you have pushed your stone to the top of the mountain, you find there is another one, taller than Everest, staring you in the face.

I do think I have written about some of the more

important series and, through the series, dealt with the most significant genres on television. Using each program or series as a point of departure, I've tried to say something about each genre—that is, each *kind* of program: westerns, situation comedies, news programs, sports programs, spectaculars, and space operas, among others.

*What this chapter represents is an inquiry, on my part, into what it is I've discovered:* what themes keep popping up in my analyses, what values do the programs espouse in common (to the extent that they do keep on being repeated), what problems do the programs wrestle with? What generalizations emerge from this small but hopefully representative sampling of American television? We've looked at the trees. Now, what does the forest look like?

I decided to write this summary because of an experience I had with my book *The Comic-Stripped American*. I discovered, when I got the courage to reread it (after all the bother with proofs and such it becomes very hard to look at one's books), that there were some informing themes in it that I had not been aware of. I had been asked to write an essay on comics and wrote what was, in effect, a summary of these themes, what could have been a summary chapter for *The Comic-Stripped American*. It is perfectly reasonable for me to be unaware of important aspects of one's own work; after all, I assume that there are all kinds of hidden messages in comics and television, and writers and all people are generally unaware of the full significance and real meanings of their acts. The same applies to myself.

But I can, at least, identify matters that come to the surface in the various chapters, and that is what I have done in the next section.

The first topic that I would like to discuss is a rather

abstract one and deals more with the structure of the programs than the content. I am talking about a constantly appearing binary structure, which takes many different forms: oppositions of a philosophic and moral nature as in *Kung Fu*; the alternating self theme in the *Star Trek* adventure I described; or the multiple oppositions described in the *Gunsmoke* episode.

As I reviewed my essays on the various programs I wrote about, I was struck by the oppositional nature of many of the themes and plots. I have suggested in the chapter on *Kung Fu* that there is a dialectic that exists in the American mind. We define ourselves in "contrast to" other cultures—Europe, or in this case, the East. In this particular case, the intellectual structure of the program, which involves the reconciliation of opposites, deals with another central theme—identity, which I will discuss later. The *Gunsmoke* adventure involved solving the paradox of the natural community, and that may also be the central problem of the Western. How does an individual situate himself in the world when he cannot remain outside of society, since he is a social being, and cannot stand the restraints and moral compromises caused by living in society?

It may be that paradox, the conflict between opposites* which seem to contradict one another but which, in reality, expresses truth—paradox and the binary structure involved in paradox—may be constituents of all thinking, a universal structure in the mind. Whatever the case, parodox seems to be vitally important in enriching our lives. As a psychiatrist, William Fry, Jr., has written in *Sweet Madness*:

---

* Admittedly, I am using paradox in a rather special way here—focusing upon the notion that it is involved with oppositions of one sort or another.

. . . the presence of paradox seems to add much richness to life. Mentioned so far is paradox in play, ritual, dreams, folklore, fantasy, art, drama, psychotherapy, and humor. These phenomena include much human creativity. A large part of that which comforts and affords pleasure in human life is encompassed in these categories. Paradox appears to be centrally vital in all of them.

If paradox is, then, central to so much of our thinking, it is the nature of the specific oppositions that must be investigated. American television programs will reflect American culture and deal with issues important to Americans.

Let me offer one example in passing. In a fascinating essay, "Who is More Dry: Heroes of Japanese Youth," Robert Lifton compares two films—*The Seven Samurai,* and its American imitation, *The Magnificent Seven.* He determines that the films reflect important value configurations in their respective cultures and, as might be expected, are considerably different from one another in terms of the values they reflect. The essay really deals with different cultural identities, and it is to identity, an important subject but a difficult one to deal with, that I would like to turn now. I say it is hard to come to grips with identity with good reason; there are few subjects that are more ambiguous and diffuse, meaning so many different things to different people —and there is no subject that is more central and immediate to people than identity.

Though I had no intention of focusing upon the subject of identity or, if you will, the problem of identity, it pervades the essays. There is, I believe, a link between the American antihistorical attitude, which leads to our seeing ourselves as what I have called "spiritual orphans," and our fascination and maybe even obsession with our identity.

People who grow up in societies with rich historical traditions and strongly entrenched customs and rites of passage do not have to worry about who they are, how to "define" themselves. They are constantly told this. It is only when you have an abstract society, when you escape from history, when people are anonymous and depersonalized, that identity becomes problematical.

Think of the difference between the inhabitants of the monastery in *Kung Fu* and the typical American. In this particular case Caine will serve as a typical case study of an immigrant with a secure identity while in the old country and an amorphous one in America. The Chinese monastery provided structure which, in turn, led to self-definition. Everyone knew who he was, where he belonged in the Great Chain of Being, what he could expect and what he must do.

This does not mean, however, that people there—or in any structured society—lacked autonomy; far from it. It is in America, where there is so little to confirm identity, that people struggle to "know themselves." Our individualism has been an acid, which has made it almost impossible to obtain community, for masterless men are inherently antisocial. The relationship between structure and autonomy has been discussed by Dorothy Lee in *Freedom and Culture*:

> Many people in our society have been apprehensive of the implications of personal autonomy, because they have felt that it is apt to lead to lawlessness and chaos. Yet actually it is in connection with the highest personal autonomy that we often find the most intricately developed structure; and it is this structure that makes autonomy possible in a group situation.

It is when you have a structural vacuum that difficulties

involving freedom and identity arise, and the preoccupation with identity that I have found in so many of the television programs and series is an indicator of an important social problem.

For instance, the series *Mission Impossible* dealt with identity in many of its episodes. In this series, which had a very definite identity of its own (with highly ritualized beginnings and endings), characters impersonate other people, masks are commonly worn, and deception is a basic category. Identity is portrayed as very loose, something that can be easily appropriated by others, and even the bureaucratic paraphernalia of identity cannot safeguard one's identity. The team in *Mission Impossible* can doctor records with consummate ease; they strip off their rubber masks at the end of their adventures and reveal to us that we can take little for granted as far as identity is concerned. Everyone can be deceived; anyone can be impersonated.

The lack of historical consciousness in America (as I have explained matters), the notion we have that in escaping from history and traditions and institutions we have attained freedom, is an illusion. For the irony is that in escaping from "restrictions" of a social nature, we become victimized by our own inhibitions, feelings of guilt and anxieties, and they are frequently more severe and more confining than ones we find in a traditional and historically based society. We tend to be more severe with ourselves than society would be; self-censorship is always more rigorous than censorship imposed from without. There is probably more status anxiety in America, where lines are not well delineated, than in European societies, where they are. The same can be said of anxiety about one's identity. In *Upstairs-Downstairs*, for example, the characters are all beauti-

fully defined and the question of identity is of little consequence—until, that is, the union of upstairs and downstairs creates complications.

In addition to problems of personal identity, and closely connected with it, is the matter of national identity, or national character, if you will. The two phenomena are part of the same problem and what we do when we discuss personal or national identity is either to narrow or widen our focus. In dealing with characters in the various television programs the focus has been on personality traits of the characters, but it has been impossible to separate such matters from the cultural ambience in which they find themselves. I assume that there are certain behavior patterns and values which are dominant in American culture and that these traits and values will "inform" the various programs. As the saying goes, "You can take the boy out of Brooklyn but you can't take the Brooklyn out of the boy."

It is only logical, then, to find many of our concerns being reflected in television. Should it surprise us, in a society that puts a premium on youthfulness, to have heroes who are innocent, young, adolescent in certain cases, and sometimes even infantile? In England, one of the most popular children's programs was *Dr. Who*—and while I was there the actor who played Dr. Who must have been in his late fifties or early sixties. A real father figure. He is involved in all kinds of bizarre adventures, often of a futuristic, science-fictional nature, and has the same campy nature that Batman has, though in a more subtle manner. He wears Victorian dress and is revealed to be a time traveller, a man who has existed all through history and who knew everyone of consequence in history. Dr. Who, then, is antithetical to the essential American hero, a figure who has no history,

who is young and perhaps even an orphan. In England people do not believe in the moral superiority of the adolescent and that little children will lead them. Innocence and naiveté are not the basic ingredients in the hero from an historical society, as they tend to be in America.

Analyzing the collective daydreams of a culture is a trying and risky task. The arts—whether elite or popular —do not lend themselves to rigorous sociological study, and culture criticism has the quality of being at once suggestive and highly speculative. My personal inclinations—and I should imagine this must be obvious to my readers—are to take risks, to offer generalizations, which I think are useful and revealing. All I can hope is that you found this book stimulating and entertaining in the best sense of the word —namely, that you were introduced to ideas and conceptions that you had not thought of before.

# afterword

I believe that television is the most important socializing force in America, but instead of being our servant it has become our master. It feeds upon our alienation, intensifying and reinforcing it. It organizes our lives, creating, in subtle ways, a reign of terror. God forbid someone cannot afford one of the treasures it holds up before us. "See," it tells us, "what you can have. . . ." implying that a life of ceaseless consumption is our *raison d'etre*. "See what life is like," it says, and parades before us a succession of murderers and hunters of murderers, moral grotesques, nitwits, fools, and clowns.

The more we watch it the more disassociated from life we become, the more abstract. We finally become cruel per-

versions of the hero Emerson talked about in *Nature*. His hero could exclaim, passionately:

> I become a transparent eyeball; I am nothing, I see all

But this was in the context of a person "standing on the bare ground" and feeling an identity with God through nature. His hero is in the woods communing with God. We have sloughed off our bodies and become videofreaks, who see all and are nothing, who want all and have (we are led to feel) nothing.

I believe that television is on too many hours and that the quality has been diluted too greatly. No medium should monopolize our time the way television does—it is not healthy. It is a narcotic, which helps assuage our loneliness and yet, which reinforces it. You cannot divorce a medium from the society in which it flourishes and if statistics I have seen are correct, and the typical American spends something like seven hours per day *alone,* then it is our social structure that must be indicted as well as television. I feel a sense of great compassion for all the bored and lonely people (mostly women) exposed to the mind-rot of afternoon television programming, which I find particularly offensive.

The tragedy of television is that it is too much in the control of businessmen and not enough in the control of artists and writers. It exists now primarily as a means for carrying commercials and programs that attract viewers so they can be exposed to commercials. Everything has been turned upside down, and the American public, which owns the airwaves (they are public property), is victimized by hucksterism of the most irritating and destructive nature. Personally speaking, I find commercials so painful that I find it hard to watch commercial television, which is not

free by any means. We all "pay" for the programs when we purchase advertised products.

We find ourselves immersed, here, in a very complicated problem, for "control" of television involves politics and aesthetics and God knows what else. How does one avoid turning a medium into an instrument of propaganda for the state? How does one "liberate" the creative talent of the brilliant actors, directors, producers, and writers we have? How does one deal with the problem of mass taste? How does one finance television? Since all of these problems are interrelated, any time you get involved in what might be called "the culture question," you find yourself trying to unravel a Gordian knot—and where is the Alexander the Great to offer us an answer?

It may be that we are looking in the wrong place and that changes in television will flow from changes taking place in society in general. If so, then it is not too extravagant to envision a situation in which social revolution will set the stage for cultural revolution, leading to a restructuring of the television industry and its utilization as a means of stimulating self-development and raising consciousness, and not as a means of exploitation. If television and the culture industries only give people "what they want," then perhaps developments in society, which may even be influenced by television, will force the issue. For television requires an audience, and if we become Hippies and "turn off" then it will have to make adjustments. And new technological developments may enable all of us to become producers and artists on cable systems. The rise in the educational level of the public also will have some influence— as will the reemergence of the whole culture question.

Television is now twenty-five years old. It's a mirror

of our culture, which has the strange power to affect it, in the same way that our image in the mirror gives us a sense of who we are, which has an influence on the way we act. In another twenty-five years I hope we will find a different kind of television existing in a different social ambience. There will no longer be commercials and the airwaves will no longer be filled with brutalizing violence and mind-deadening pap. The creative people in the industry will be freed from bondage to ratings and hucksters and television will realize its potentialities.

There must be some way to mediate between the extremes of television as an instrument of state mind-control and the anarchy of commercialized brainwashing that currently exists. There must be some way to avoid the boring television found in some societies and the frenetic, junk-filled (but lively) television found in America. Must the video screen choose between "uplifting" material to bring elite culture to the masses or vile or brutalizing junk to lower the cultural level of the populace? Do we have to choose between sermons and violent deaths at the hands of monsters and murderers?

I think there are alternatives to the extremes sketched above and hope we can find them. Of course I write as a moralist who believes that we must make changes in television of considerable magnitude if we are to maintain our collective sanity. If we merely get more of the same on the video screen we will probably perish in a chaos of demented visions of ourselves and our possibilities.

# acknowledgments

Anyone who writes a book owes debts of one sort or another to all kinds of people. My wife, Phyllis, and my children, Miriam and Gabriel, put up with a lot of nonsense from me while I was writing this book. My children found it somewhat bizarre watching television with me, while I scribbled away, furiously, in a notebook, and my wife had to listen to all my devious explanations and analyses of what I had seen on television. I am grateful to them for their infinite patience. The book was written at the suggestion of Linda McDermott of Walker and Company. I appreciate her guidance and encouragement as well as the actual editing by Patricia Aks and Wilson Gathings.

I have been described as an "armchair psychoanalyst"

(what other kinds are there?) of popular culture and, quite naturally, I owe a great deal to people in this school who have given me ideas and modes of interpreting my material. Thus I have benefited from reading work by Sigmund Freud, Martin Grotjahn, Herbert Hendin, Bronislaw Malinowski, Erik H. Erikson, Ernest Dichter, Carl G. Jung, Alan Dundes, Erich Fromm, Theodore Reik, and Geoffrey Gorer, as well as many others mining this rich vein. I have also been influenced by the work of Edgar Morin, Roland Barthes, Umberto Eco, Jean-Marie Benoist, John Cawelti, Mircea Eliade, David Manning White, Ray Brown, Orrin Klapp, Richard Hoggart, Charles Winick, Franco Ferrarotti, Erving Goffman, Alan Gowans, Harold Garfinkle, Henri Lefebvre, and Johan Huizinga.

My analysis of American culture leans heavily on the work of people such as David Noble, Mulford Sibley, John William Ward, Philip Slater, W. Lloyd Warner, Marshall Fishwick, R. W. B. Lewis, and Leslie Fiedler. There are many other scholars and writers, sociologists, folklorists, artists, anthropologists, psychiatrists, literary critics, novelists—I could go on much longer—whose work has been meaningful and useful to me.

Finally, I have benefited from the friendship of a number of people whose kindness and helpfulness I appreciate. My brother, Jason; my sister-in-law, Marilyn Powers; and my nephew, Adam, have always been a source of inspiration to me. I also owe debts of gratitude to George Gerbner, William Porter, Aaron Wildavsky, Harry Geduld, William Fry, Jr., Warren Bennis, S. I. Hayakawa, Matti Kuusi, Irving Louis Horowitz, Stan Lee, Charles Schulz, Jackson Gregory Savelle, and Marshall Lumsden, for kind letters, favors, and good jokes, among other things.

The Faculty Manuscript Service at San Francisco State University typed the manuscript for this book with patience and conscientiousness.

Grateful acknowledgment is made to the following publishers and authors for permission to use copyrighted material from their works:

Pierre Bourdieu, "Systems of Education and Systems of Thought."

Barry Cole, *Television*. Free Press, New York, 1970.

Committee on Children's Television, *Children's Television Fact Sheet*. April 25, 1971.

John Cawelti, *The Six-Gun Mystique,* Bowling Green University Popular Press, 1971.

Walter Cronkite, "What It's Like to Broadcast News," *Saturday Review,* Dec. 12, 1970.

Ignatius Donnelly, *Caesar's Column,* edited by Walter B. Rickout. The Belknap Press of Harvard University Press, 1960 (originally published 1890).

*The Selected Writings of Ralph Waldo Emerson,* edited with a biographical introduction by Brooks Atkinson, The Modern Library, 1960.

Martin Grotjahn, M. D., *Beyond Laughter,* McGraw-Hill, 1957.

Stuart Hall and Paddy Whannel, *The Popular Arts: A Critical Guide to the Mass Media,* Copyright © 1964, Pantheon Books.

Peter Lennon, *The Sunday Times,* London, Sept. 16, 1973.

R. W. B. Lewis, *The American Adam,* Phoenix Books, 1955.

Excerpt from *Political Man* by Seymour Martin Lipset. Copyright © 1959, 1960 by Seymour Martin Lipset. Used by permission of Doubleday & Company, Inc.

Karl Mannheim, *Ideology and Utopia,* Harcourt Brace Jovanovich, Inc., 1936.

Newsweek, Inc.: "Rhoda: A Star Is Spun Off," Oct. 7, 1974. "TV Speaking About the Unspeakable," Nov. 29, 1971. Reprinted by permission.

Dwight Newton, *S. F. Sunday Examiner.*

Quote on Warren E. Burger © 1971 by the New York Times Company. Reprinted by permission.

Sally Quinn, *The Washington Post.*

Michael R. Real, "Super Bowl: Mythic Spectacle," *Journal of Communication,* Winter 1975.

Rex Reed, *New York News.*

Milton R. Sapirstein, *Paradoxes of Everyday Life,* copyright © Random House, 1955.

Alberta Siegel, "Mass Media Violence: Effects on Children," *Stanford M.D.*

*Time,* The Weekly Newsmagazine: "The Prinze of Prime Time," Sept. 30, 1974. Reprinted by permission. Copyright Time Inc.

"Upstairs-Downstairs," published by permission of Transaction, Inc., from *Society,* volume 12, #4. Copyright © 1975, by Transaction, Inc.

Neil Vidmar and Milton Rokeach, "Archie Bunker's Bigotry: A Study in Selective Perception and Exposure," *Journal of Communication,* Winter 1974.

Scott Ward, Harvard University Graduate School of Business Administration, "Effects of Television Advertising on Adolescents: Preliminary Research Results."